First Steps to Literacy

LIBRARY PROGRAMS FOR PARENTS, TEACHERS, AND CAREGIVERS

prepared by

*The Preschool Services
and Parent Education Committee*

*Association for Library Service
to Children*

AMERICAN LIBRARY ASSOCIATION

Chicago and London

1990

Preschool Services and Parent Education Committee
Association for Library Service to Children

Members of the Preschool Services and Parent Education Committee, during the years 1985–1989, who contributed to this book are

Caroline Feller Bauer, author and lecturer, Huntington Beach, California

Nell Colburn, Prince George's County Memorial Library System, Hyattsville, Maryland

Floyd Dickman, State Library of Ohio, Columbus, Ohio

Maralita L. Freeny, Prince George's County Memorial Library System, Hyattsville, Maryland

Harriet Herschel, King County Library System, Seattle, Washington

Sue McCleaf-Nespeca, NOLA Regional Library System, Youngstown, Ohio

Cynthia K. Richey, Mt. Lebanon Public Library, Pittsburgh, Pennsylvania

Cover and text designed by Charles Bozett.

Composed by ALA Books/Publishing Services on a BestInfo Wave4 pre-press system and output on a Linotronic L-300 in New Caledonia by Anzo Graphics.

Printed on 50-pound Glatfelter B-16, a pH-neutral stock and bound in 10-point Carolina cover stock by Port City Press, Inc.

The paper used in this publication meets the minimum requirements of American National Standard for Information Sciences — Permanence of Paper for Printed Library Materials, ANSI Z39.48-1984. ♾

Printed in the United States of America.

94 93 92 91 90   5 4 3 2 1

Contents

Introduction   v

Choosing and Using Books for the Youngest Children   1

Programming, Planning, and Presentation   13

Seven Library Programs   29

    First Books for Your Baby   29

    Raising Reading Children   32

    Books Alive! Sharing Books with Young Children   47

    Start with a Story: Circle Time for Preschoolers   56

    Gift Books for Young Children   70

    Power of Books: Using Literature in the Religious Education
       of Young Children   75

    Finding Picture Books for Special Needs   87

Subject Index   97

Title Index   101

Introduction

This book is a response to a mandate given to the nation's children's librarians by their professional colleagues. In 1984 the American Library Association issued *Realities: Educational Reform in a Learning Society*,[1] which addresses the dramatic findings of the National Commission on Excellence in Education in its landmark report, *A Nation at Risk: The Imperative for Educational Reform*.[2]

In *Realities*, ALA underlines the importance of the public library's role in preschool learning: "Libraries contribute to preschool learning in two ways: through the services, programs and materials that help parents increase their skills and capabilities, and through programs that serve children directly."[3]

Calling upon public officials to appropriate funds for parent education and early childhood services in the public library, *Realities* points out that "parents, volunteers and day care staff learn from librarians how to select and use materials with children. Librarians have the skills, experience, and desire to conduct workshops for parents, older children, babysitters, early childhood specialists, teachers and volunteers."[4]

The Preschool Services and Parent Education Committee regards these statements as a mandate: traditional public library programming for children must be supplemented with programming for parents, caregivers, and other adults who live or work with preschool children.

The Committee believes that children's librarians have a unique knowledge and expertise—a knowledge of the varied literature available for chil-

1. *Realities: Educational Reform in a Learning Society*. A statement by the American Library Association Task Force on Excellence in Education (Chicago: American Library Association, 1984).
2. *A Nation at Risk: The Imperative for Educational Reform*. A Report to the Nation and the Secretary of Education, United States Department of Education, by the National Commission on Excellence in Education (Washington, D.C.: Government Printing Office, 1983).
3. *Realities*, 3.
4. Ibid.

dren today; an expertise in techniques for making this literature an integral part of children's daily lives. Who knows children's books—and recordings and films and songs and rhymes and games—better than the children's librarian? Who else sees such a large percentage of the best books published for children each year? Who else knows the most successful ones to use with groups of children—the best to use with two-year-olds, with four-year-olds, with beginning readers? Who can best recommend a book for the three-year-old who is expecting a new sibling, for the four-year-old who has lost a beloved grandparent, for the five-year-old who is moving? And who knows best how to extend the literary experience with flannel boards, with puppets, with creative dramatics?

Children's librarians know the books, and they know how to give children exciting, memorable experiences with them. Research indicates that it is these experiences that make readers. A child must want to read before he or she will make the effort to learn to read.

Children cannot discover the delights of books on their own. They need an adult to bring books into their lives and help them discover that books and reading are fun. The adult is the vital link between children and the world of books; the children's librarian is the vital link between thousands of adults and the children for whom they care.

The Preschool Services and Parent Education Committee believes that children's librarians have an obligation to share their expertise with parents and the growing community of adults who work with young children. Library programs that encourage adults to bring children and books together are the first steps toward a literate society.

The Committee has designed this book to aid children's librarians in extending their traditional library programming to include adults. Drawing on the experiences of children's librarians who have already become involved in adult programming, the book details seven successful programs in readable, easy-to-use outline format. These programs were presented to parents, grandparents, expectant parents, family caregivers, preschool teachers, child care center personnel, high school students, religious educators, and library staffs.

The Committee invites librarians to use these programs and accompanying bibliographies as they appear here or to tailor them to fit their community's needs or their own special tastes and interests.

Hours of careful preparation went into each of the presentations, and each was reworked again and again in response to participants' feedback. A chapter on successful program planning pulls together the experience of the librarians who designed the programs. It offers strategies for targeting an adult audience and aggressively publicizing a program, suggestions for selecting an effective site, ideas for preparing intriguing bibliographies, and methods for successful program evaluation.

Another chapter addresses the contributors' discovery that the audiences for these library programs are often composed of adults who live and work with babies and very young children. The chapter provides an overview of the literature available for use with infants and children through age three and offers suggestions for choosing books and using them at specific stages of child development.

The Committee is especially pleased to note that although all the programs were originally planned for specific audiences, each is multi-purpose. Moreover, the programs have interchangeable parts. Harriet Herschel's "Start With a Story: Circle Time for Preschoolers" was first presented to high school students; but it would be equally effective as a short program for child care center personnel, family caregivers, or library volunteers. Sue McCleaf-Nespeca often presents a longer version of Herschel's program. In a three-hour presentation intended for early childhood educators, McCleaf-Nespeca devotes an hour or so to the basics of reading aloud and storytelling for preschoolers; she then booktalks titles that she feels would be of special interest to her audience. The extensive bibliographies from which McCleaf-Nespeca draws her booktalks are appended to Herschel's basic talk. The two programs could be combined nicely into a long, one-day program or a series of weekly or monthly ones.

Readers will find a similar relationship between Herschel's "Finding Picture Books for Special Needs" and Maralita Freeny's "Power of Books: Using Literature in the Religious Education of Young Children." Herschel takes a simple, short approach that is really a series of booktalks. It would be an ideal program for a children's librarian who is a confident booktalker but who has not yet programmed for adults. Librarians with more experience will feel comfortable with Freeny's ambitious approach. Titles and subjects from the two talks are readily interchangeable.

Caroline Feller Bauer's enthusiastic overview of books for babies will be as useful for family caregivers and students in child care classes as for expectant parents. For more suggestions on programming for expectant parents, investigate the first sections of Nell Colburn's "Books Alive! Sharing Books with Young Children" or Freeny's "Raising Reading Children."

While each of the programs has a different emphasis, all have a common purpose—to encourage adults to seek out the best books and put them into the hands of the children they love.

NELL COLBURN

Choosing and Using Books for the Youngest Children

NELL COLBURN

The children's librarians contributing to this book have found that the adults who attend their programs have two basic interests. Whether they are parents, caregivers, religious educators, grandparents, or preschool teachers, they want to know *how to choose* and *how to use*. They want to know how to choose a book for a child and how to match a particular child or group of children with an appropriate book. And they want to know how to use books with children; they want to know how they can make books come alive for children the way children's librarians do.

One particularly noticeable trend has intrigued all of the contributors: people are asking about books for their children at an earlier stage than ever before. They come into libraries and look at the shelves and shelves of picture books and ask, "Where do I start?" More and more of them are aware that reading aloud to their children will make a difference; they realize that children need entertaining and memorable experiences with books if they are to become readers; and they recognize the value of an early start. They are enthusiastic, but they often are baffled: "How does one actually use a book with an infant?" they ask. Or they are frustrated: "My baby used to enjoy books, but now she's impossible. She just wants to grab every book in sight and tear it to pieces!" Or they are inexperienced: "At our day care center we have a story time for four- and five-year-olds; I'd like to do something for the twos and threes, but their attention spans are so short!"

Most children's librarians have developed expertise in choosing books for and using them with three- to five-year-olds, the traditional preschool story time audience. But few librarians have the confidence with babies and very young children that they have with the older preschoolers. This is perhaps because many of them are just discovering how much material for very young children they have in their collections, or they are just beginning to extend library programming to a younger age group.

This chapter provides an overview of books for very young children—infants through age three—and offers suggestions for using these books

1

with young children at different stages of their development. It is offered as background reading for librarians with the expectation that more of them will be asked to program for adults who want to use books with the very young. Two strong beliefs guide this overview: it is never too early to give a child a book; and it is a child's individual stage of development, not chronological age, that is most important when matching a child with a book.

Nursery Rhymes and Songs

Collections of nursery rhymes and songs are the first books to bring into a new baby's world. They yield lullabies, good morning songs, songs for crib play, and rhymes to match the routines that mark every new baby's day. These books offer parents and caregivers the opportunity to share a delightful heritage with their children, the heritage of a rich oral literature that has been passed down through generations of parents and their children.

New babies cannot lift their heads or focus their eyes to experience the visual pleasures of books; they cannot understand the sense of words. But from birth they are enchanted with language, and they thrive on words as they grow.

Nursery rhymes and songs are a delightful way to introduce babies to words and to the exciting sounds and rhythms of our language. Words are the tools that a child uses for thinking and communicating with others. A child who hears a lot of words will learn a lot of words. And a child who learns a lot of words will speak well, think clearly, and grow to be a good listener. All of this will add up to a child's becoming a good reader. Specialists in reading education have found that it is important to expose a child to a variety of words during early years. Tiny babies will not understand the words of a nursery rhyme any more than they will understand all the other words adults share daily. That understanding will come in time. Meanwhile, baby will love the sing-song nature of the rhymes and songs and will begin to develop a feeling for the patterns of speech. A baby who hears, "Baa, baa, black sheep, have you any wool?" is hearing how a question is phrased. And a baby who hears "Yes, sir, yes sir, three bags full!" is hearing how a question is answered.

MOTHER GOOSE

The most comprehensive collections of traditional nursery rhymes available today are often labeled Mother Goose rhymes. Scholars disagree about who Mother Goose was, but the name has been associated with folk stories and traditional verse for young children in France, Britain, and the United States for two centuries.

The lasting appeal of Mother Goose may be that the subjects of the rhymes come straight out of a baby's everyday world. The rhymes are concerned with getting up in the morning, getting dressed, going to the market, cooking, eating, coping with the weather. It's fun to match these rhymes with the events in a baby's day. "Rub-a-Dub-Dub" is a good choice for baby's bath time; "One, Two, Buckle My Shoe" can make dressing a young child a game rather than a struggle.

Mother Goose rhymes are full of wonderful words. Many of the rhymes reinforce words that a child hears in daily conversation—tub, rain, up, down, shoe, bake, fall. By introducing less familiar, but good, strong words—contrary, blithe, horrid, crooked, delve, tattered, dainty, nimble— lots of the rhymes will strengthen and stretch any child's vocabulary.

Much of the charm of the Mother Goose rhymes comes from their use of onomatopoeia and alliteration. Adults as well as children take pleasure in such phrases as "silver bells and cockle shells," "one misty-moisty morning," "daffydown-dilly," and a "peck of pickled peppers." A child who is exposed to such language will grow up with a natural appreciation for poetry and for language used well.

Some of the world's most talented artists have illustrated collections of Mother Goose rhymes. Many beautiful books are available in a fascinating array of artistic interpretations. Librarians will want to have a variety on their shelves—Brian Wildsmith's rich watercolors of medieval origin; Raymond Briggs' lively, humorous little scenes; Blanche Fisher Wright's homey folk in old-fashioned dress; Marguerite de Angeli's finely detailed, gentle watercolors; Tomie dePaola's exuberant, folksy characters; Arnold Lobel's colorful, droll interpretation.

A collection that includes a large number and a wide variety of familiar and less well-known rhymes and provides a first line index is a solid first purchase for either a library or a home bookshelf.

When introducing Mother Goose books, librarians may want to:

Invite new and expectant parents, grandparents, and other gift-givers to a show-and-tell discussion of the variety of Mother Goose collections available. Encourage adults to browse through the library's collections of Mother Goose and choose the work of an illustrator they like. Their tastes should determine the choice of a first Mother Goose book because adults are more likely to use the book with children if they find the illustrations appealing.

Encourage adults to introduce rhymes even before their children are old enough to sit on their laps and listen and look. The rhymes are easy to learn and to share with babies, and they are so much fun to say when the right occasion arises; librarians can point out rhymes appropriate for daily routines such as getting dressed, taking a nap, and bathing.

Plan a series of short Mother Goose programs for parents and young children. Read a book about bath time, getting dressed, or going to market, and follow up with appropriate Mother Goose rhymes, perhaps making them into action rhymes or games. Be sure to have a selection of Mother Goose books to browse through and checkout, and encourage parents to repeat the rhymes and activities at home. Programs like this are more for adults than their little ones, although everyone goes away satisfied.

Encourage adults to continue to checkout Mother Goose collections as their children grow and become more able to appreciate different artistic interpretations of old friends such as Humpty Dumpty or Little Bo-Peep. Librarians can encourage adults to ask their children to talk about the picture of Humpty they like best and explain why they like it. Such experiences encourage critical thinking and are much more fun for older preschoolers than most of the dull "let's talk about this" picture books that some publishers are producing in quantity today.

PLAY RHYMES

"This Little Pig Went to Market" is a traditional nursery rhyme for counting baby's toes. It has delighted many generations of babies and parents. But it is probably the only "toe counting" rhyme in most adult's repertoires. That is a shame, because countries all over the world have rhymes for baby play in their literature—rhymes for toe counting, knee bouncing, hand clapping, leg wagging, foot patting, face tapping, and tickling.

Terms such as toe counting come from a delightful book called *This Little Pig Went to Market: Play Rhymes for Infants and Young Children*, by Norah Montgomerie. First published in 1966 by The Bodley Head in London, it was reprinted in 1970 and 1975 and issued in a new edition in 1983. It is a treasure trove of verse culled from the rich body of rhymes in English literature. Here, parents will find nine toe counting rhymes and seven alternatives to the popular hand clapping rhyme, "Pat-a-Cake," as well as a marvelous assortment of face tapping rhymes and lively tickles to use with babies in a crib or on a lap. For older babies who enjoy a rollicking ride on a grown-up's knee, there are twenty-five knee bouncing, or jig jog rhymes.

The best thing about this book is that Montgomerie gives clear, easy-to-follow directions for adding actions to each rhyme. As she explains in her introduction, the actions used with each rhyme illustrate the abstract words or concepts for a baby more clearly than any picture could.

In 1955 Iona and Peter Opie of Great Britain produced the classic source book of these rhymes, *The Oxford Nursery Rhyme Book*. Librarians will want a copy of this excellent collection as a reference tool. But the book will not be attractive to most parents and caregivers because of the almost overwhelming number of rhymes, the small print, the sparse directions, and the small black-and-white illustrations, selected from eighteenth and nineteenth century toy books and chapbooks. Perhaps the recent interest in books for babies will encourage publishers to produce more collections of rhymes as accessible as Montgomerie's.

Perhaps there will also be more collections of nursery rhymes from non-English-speaking cultures. In her book *The Laughing Baby: Remembering Nursery Rhymes and Reasons*, Ann Scott offers a small selection of play rhymes from a number of countries, including the Ivory Coast, the Soviet Union, Japan, India, and Colombia.

Most useful to librarians, parents, and caregivers are collections with:

A large, but not imposing number of rhymes from both English and non-English-speaking countries.

Medium-sized print that can be read easily from a slight distance.

Appealing, instructive illustrations featuring children of many ethnic origins.

Simple, clear directions for adding actions to each rhyme.

When introducing rhyme books in the library's collection, librarians may want to:

Demonstrate the actions for the play rhymes with the help of a child or by using a doll or stuffed animal if a child is not available.

Introduce books such as Clyde and Wendy Watson's *Father Fox's Pennyrhymes* and *Catch Me and Kiss Me and Say It Again*. These are engaging collections of original nursery rhymes, but they do not include suggestions for accompanying play actions. Once adults have caught on to the idea of using actions with rhymes, they will appreciate books like these more.

Encourage adults to learn some of the rhymes by heart, perhaps by demonstrating just how easy this is in a program.

Use the rhymes in library programs for young children, connecting them thematically with picture books.

SONG BOOKS

Songs are a wonderful way to speak to a baby. They can seem almost magical as they calm children or make them laugh.

A good library collection will have a selection of song books, which include lullabies, good morning songs, and songs for interactive play throughout the day. A comprehensive collection such as Marie Winn's *The Fireside Book of Children's Songs* or Jane Hart and Anita Lobel's *Singing Bee! A Collection of Favorite Children's Songs* will help adults remember the words to their favorite childhood songs and introduce many new ones as well. Also useful is a book like Tom Glazer's *Eye Winker, Tom Tinker, Chin Chopper: Fifty Musical Fingerplays*, which provides a selection of songs for crib play with babies. Glazer explains how to please a baby by using actions to accompany songs like "Pop Goes the Weasel" and "Where Is Thumbkin." Even the tiniest baby will respond with smiles and gurgles, with waving hands or kicking feet.

These nursery songs offer another first experience with poetry. Like the Mother Goose rhymes, much of their pleasure comes from the sound of the words, from alliteration, onomatopoeia, and repetition. They offer the child a wonderful variety of words and images and give a sense of the patterns of our language. "Where is Thumbkin?" asks a question; "Here I am!" is the answer.

Many of the songs provide a first encounter with basic concepts. "This Old Man" is a popular song for learning numbers. It may not teach counting, but it will acquaint young children with the idea of numbers and make them more comfortable with the concept. Lots of songs emphasize body parts. "Put Your Finger in the Air" is an especially catchy example, popular with babies, toddlers, and even five-year-olds. Everyone enjoys putting fingers on heads, noses, chins, and cheeks—or even better, seeing mom, dad or big sister do it!

A basic song book should offer a large number as well as a wide variety of songs. Most adults need the words to traditional songs, because they remember them only in part from their childhoods. A book offering a solid selection of traditional songs as well as some less familiar ones is a good choice, as is one with a range of selections, from good morning songs to lullabies, from lively action game songs to quiet, soothing verses for nap time. More than one verse of a song should be included. If actions are suggested, they should be simple and clearly explained. A title index, or an alternative such as the alphabetically arranged table of contents in Tom Glazer's book is necessary. A subject index is also useful. Piano music should be included; many preschool teachers appreciate guitar chords as well. Musical arrangements should be easy to play and offered in a singable key.

When introducing song books in the collection, librarians may want to:

Demonstrate a variety of songs—especially those for crib play—with accompanying actions.

Encourage parents to substitute their own children's names in songs such as "Lazy Mary, will you get up?"

Encourage parents to learn songs so that music is readily available when needed—to pass time during a traffic jam; for soothing a child after a fall; for quieting a boisterous group of two-year-olds.

Demonstrate how many of the songs connect thematically with books in the library's collection.

Demonstrate how many good song books grow along with children as they offer delightful singing games appropriate for older preschoolers, such as "Bingo," "The Noble Duke of York," "John Brown's Baby," and "John Jacob Jinglehamer Schmidt." Caregivers and preschool teachers especially appreciate programs that highlight songs appropriate for groups of children.

Picture Books for Babies

During the first two months of life, as babies become able to lift their heads for longer and longer periods, they will be excited by picture books with bright colors and simple shapes. These books can be opened out and stood up on shelves or furniture in the nursery. Some of the sturdier ones can be placed in a crib or playpen. If the book has cardboard pages, it can stand on its own; if its pages are paper, rubberbands can hold it open to a certain place. Introducing attractive books in a child's home environment right from the start makes the statement that books are an important and necessary part of life. Children are likely to continue to associate books with pleasure throughout their childhoods if books contribute enjoyment during their first days, weeks, and months in the world.

The best picture books for crib and nursery display are those in which the emphasis is on illustration rather than text. Illustrations should be crisp and uncluttered, with bold lines for the child to focus on easily. Babies seem to prefer bright, contrasting colors to soft pastels. They also prefer intriguing patterns to solid colors. Bill Martin and Eric Carle's *Brown Bear, Brown Bear, What Do You See?*, Mirra Ginsburg's *Across the Stream*, and Nancy Tafuri's *Morning, Rabbit, Morning* are good choices.

When a baby is old enough to sit on a lap, but not yet into the "grabbing and tearing" stage of infancy, their parents and caregivers will have the opportunity to discover a cozy, calm, sharing time with books, which won't come again until children near their first birthdays. During this brief period, adults and babies can enjoy simple picture books with lovely poetic texts, such as Margaret Wise Brown's beloved classic *Goodnight, Moon*.

First lap books should be short, with bright, simple illustrations and pleasing rhymes for singing or saying as the pages are turned.

Board Books

When children reach the age of four or five months, their relationship with books will change; they enter what many librarians call the grabbing and tearing stage. Children are eager now to explore their world physically, hold books and experiment with them as though they were toys, a shoe, or any other object that comes within reach. Many parents are hesitant to borrow library books for their babies at this time. Librarians should encourage them to sample the *board book* collection.

Heavy cardboard pages make board books chew resistant; many can be wiped clean. Their small size allows children with tiny hands to manipulate them easily. At approximately seven to nine months of age, children will be able to turn the pages of a board book and will begin to learn for themselves just how a book works.

In choosing board books, librarians should look for sturdy bindings and simple, bright, uncluttered illustrations. Illustrations are more important than text; a strong story line or plot is not necessary. The pictures should be lively and related to the world the child is discovering around him. Family, familiar animals, the sun, moon, rain, and daily activities, such as sleeping, getting up, getting dressed, eating, riding in the car, going for a walk are all fascinating for children during this developmental stage. Although a definite story is not necessary, good board books maintain an internal logic; the best have a subtle humor directed to the adult who must read them again and again.

Board books may seem very short and simple to adults who do not understand how to use them. They are meant to be talked about rather than read word for word. Librarians will want to demonstrate to adult groups how the pictures can be used as a springboard for conversation about colors, numbers, shapes, and the child's experiences and environment. "Oh, look," the parent might say, "that little boy is wearing a red shirt. You are wearing red today, too! Your pants are red!"

I Spy Books

As a child approaches his first birthday, adults will want to introduce *I Spy* or *naming* books. The book *I Spy* by Lucille Ogle is considered by many librarians to be the classic example of this genre. Subtitled *A Picture Book of Objects in a Child's Home Environment*, it offers simple, bright illustrations of objects, arranged according to the room where they are found—the living room, kitchen, or bedroom, for example. Ogle's introduction explains many games adults and young children can play using her book. The simplest is the basic I Spy game: "I spy a pan," the adult says, pointing to the picture of the pan. The child is then asked to locate the pan, point to it, and, if the child is old enough, say the object's name. Ogle explains many, more sophisticated ways to play the game that will enhance reading readiness skills as the child grows. Adults can use clues to stress color, shape, size, function, or number.

"I spy something green," the adult says. Then, depending on the age or stage of the child playing the game, the adult can either point to and name the green object or ask the child to do it.

To make the game harder for an older child or use it to sharpen a child's listening and observing skills, the adult may choose more difficult statements: "I spy something that is red with a green cap on it," referring to a tomato; or, "I spy something that is used to dig," referring to a shovel.

The idea is to name things, to give children words. Then, as children grow, the games can be used to develop basic reading readiness skills in a way that is fun.

Librarians may want to demonstrate some of Ogle's I Spy games and point out that they can easily be played with catalogs or magazines. Librarians might also introduce some of the many imaginative I Spy books in the library's collection, books like Peter Spier's *Gobble Growl Grunt*, Gyo Fujikawa's *A to Z Picture Book*, and Allan and Janet Ahlberg's *Peek-a-Boo!* Many adults do not understand how to share books like these with children; they need a friendly example.

Concept Books

The term *concept book* is a broad one. Many board books are simple concept books, emphasizing the alphabet or numbers. I Spy or naming books could also be considered concept books. More sophisticated picture books that explore love, friendship, and other emotional concepts are sometimes given this label. The term is used here to refer to ABC books, counting books, and books that emphasize such basic concepts as color, shape, size, opposites, and days of the week.

Concept books may be introduced sometime between a child's first and second birthday. They will become increasingly important throughout the preschool years as the child develops language skills and visual awareness and continues to make sense of the world.

Most public library collections offer a wide variety of basic concept books. Many fine illustrators have used the concept book as a medium for artistic experimentation, assuring a range of styles from which to choose.

Most concept books do not have a story line; the presentation of information is straightforward, depending on simple description or comparison. However, there are many successful concept books that rely on a narrative approach. Leo Lionni's *Little Blue and Little Yellow* and Eric Carle's *The Very Hungry Caterpillar* are two that demonstrate an imaginative use of a narrative framework.

Clarity and consistency are the most important criteria in selecting concept books. No matter what the author or illustrator's style or technique, information must be clearly and consistently presented on each page as well as from page to page. Letters and numbers should be clearly defined; objects must be easy to identify. Illustrations should relate closely to text, and once a format is established, it should be maintained throughout. For example, *x*, *y* and *z* should not be lumped together on the same page of an alphabet book if every other letter is given its own page.

Basic concept books must give special attention to the young child's needs and capabilities. A good alphabet book will portray objects with names that represent the most common sounds of letters. Blends and silent letters should be avoided. Likewise, a good alphabet book will not show a puppy on the *P* page because young children may recognize the animal as a dog, which belongs on the *D* page.

Librarians will enjoy introducing adults to the variety of concept books available. They should emphasize that while many of these books are designed for young children, others are quite sophisticated and appropriate for older preschoolers and even early elementary school students. Librarians may want to demonstrate how some concept books can be used as I Spy or naming books and as a springboards for conversation.

Short and Snappy Picture Books for Toddlers

Sometime between eighteen and thirty months of age, a child will begin to enjoy picture books with an actual story line. A good, strong, simple text is important in these books. Action is crucial. A definite plot is not necessary; the child enjoys the process of the story and relating the characters and their actions to the world. The strength of books like Eve Rice's *Benny Bakes a Cake*, John Burningham's *Mr. Gumpy's Outing*, and Donald Crews' *Freight Train* is that they have little description, which allows them to move along quickly. Illustrations continue to be important. Pictures should appear on every page, and they should always be consistent with the text.

Individual picture song books such as Aliki's *Hush Little Baby* will delight toddlers, who are just learning to sing at this stage. They will enjoy participating in the "reading" of these books and feel confident and excited by the repetitive words of the song.

Lift-the-flap books, such as Eric Hill's popular *Where's Spot?*, have the same appeal. They are designed to pull listeners right into the story by requiring their active participation.

Librarians may find that adults need their help choosing appropriate books for children at this stage more than any other time. They should encourage adults to experiment with a variety of picture books and to use a combination of reading and talking to hold the child's attention. Librarians may want to demonstrate how picture books can be paired with familiar nursery rhymes and songs or with poetry from collections such as Jack Prelutsky's *Read-Aloud Rhymes for the Very Young*.

Longer Picture Books

As their children's attention spans grow, adults will enjoy mining the wealth of the library's picture book collection. Stories with definite plots will be more satisfying to preschoolers who have become comfortable with books in their early years. Librarians should direct adults to books such as Ezra Jack Keats' *Whistle for Willie* or Gene Zion's *Harry the Dirty Dog*, which have a definite beginning, middle, and satisfying ending.

Simple information books will intrigue children as they mature and begin to explore new situations and worlds outside their immediate surroundings. Books such as Byron Barton's *Airport* and *Building a House*, Gail Gibbons' *Trucks*, and Anne Rockwell's *Fire Engines* are excellent examples that offer a clear, exciting look at a child's expanding world through a mix of words and pictures. These books invite a combination of reading and talking on a more sophisticated level.

Picture song books and participation books continue to entice children as they move beyond the simplest picture books. They encourage participation in the reading process, while drawing on a child's new verbal skills and increasing understanding of the world.

John Langstaff's *Oh, A-Hunting We Will Go* invites the child to identify animals in the pictures and match them with the rhyming verses as the song progresses. Charles Shaw's *It Looked like Spilt Milk* provides a satisfying opportunity for the child to identify the simple shapes of objects in his environment by incorporating them into a story with an irresistible, repetitive refrain.

Cumulative stories also offer an opportunity for the child's enthusiastic participation. These are stories in which a sequence of actions is repeated over and over again as the plot progresses. The child comes to understand the sequencing and begins to feel confident about joining in when the repetitive phrases are read and reread. Such participation provides a rich language experience, by exploring a variety of words and patterns of speech. Cumulative stories also encourage the child's understanding of how a story develops, the sequencing of its events. This is a crucial skill in learning to read and write. Paul Galdone's *The Gingerbread Boy*, Marjorie Flack's *Ask Mr. Bear*, and Pat Hutchins' *Goodnight, Owl* are popular examples of the cumulative story.

Adults can continue to promote basic reading readiness skills by using the library's many rhyming and wordless picture books. Bruce Degen's *Jamberry*, and other satisfying rhyming texts will help a child's vocabulary expand effortlessly. Wordless picture books, such as Jan Ormerod's *Sunshine* and John Goodall's *The Adventures of Paddy Pork*, encourage language development and logical thinking by requiring the child to tell the story in his own words.

In highlighting the longer picture books in the collection, librarians may want to:

introduce some of the well-known authors and illustrators who have produced several popular books for young children, such as people like Eve Rice, Pat Hutchins, Ezra Jack Keats, Margaret Wise Brown, Eric Carle, Tana Hoban, Byron Barton; show examples of their distinctive styles;

encourage adults to continually expose their children to a variety of artistic styles. Share ten different alphabet or counting books, talking briefly about the artwork and unique presentations of information in each book;

single out picture books on special concerns, such as the death of a pet, divorce, new baby, or hospitalization. Read several of these aloud to adult groups to demonstrate the books' warmth and sensitivity;

encourage parents to continue to read to their children as they enter school and throughout the elementary school years. Stress the importance of reading aloud as the child begins to learn to read himself. Show examples of sophisticated picture books that are meant to be read aloud to school-age children, books such as Steven Kellogg's *Pecos Bill* and Chris Van Allsburg's *Jumanji*.

Programming, Planning, and Presentation

Maralita L. Freeny

Programming for adults requires hours of careful preparation. Once you have committed yourself to the notion that you want to develop a program, there are several steps to follow that will help you plan a successful, well-attended one. Before starting an outline of the actual presentation, you will need to identify your target audience and their needs, determine the topic of the program, set goals and objectives, identify methods, and choose your location, time, and date. While this checklist may seem lengthy, attention to each factor in the first stage of planning will help ensure success.

Topics

Choose a topic with which you are comfortable. While you need not be an expert in the field, you should have experience with the topic and you need to have researched it with a degree of thoroughness. Ask yourself if you will be comfortable answering questions from the audience. If your answer is no, choose another topic. Don't sell yourself short, however. If you have had years of experience telling stories to preschoolers, you are an expert, and you should be comfortable talking to a group of teenagers or adults about how to do story time. If you have read the bulk of your library's picture book collection, used these books repeatedly in story time, and recommended them to parents, you have the background and knowledge to present a workshop on preschool literature to parents.

Another approach to choosing a topic is to base the content of your program on the needs of your community or a particular group you have targeted. In this case, you should do a needs assessment—a survey, a questionnaire, and formal or informal conversations with potential participants. Determine what topic or topics are of interest to your target audience and plan your program around those needs. This approach is especially effective when you have been invited to address a particular group. It is also helpful when planning a public program, so that you do not duplicate what is already being offered in your target area.

Audience

Before setting your goals and objectives, you must identify your potential audience. If at all possible, speak directly to them in order to identify their needs with regard to your topic. If you can address the needs of potential participants directly, people are more likely to attend. For example, you may have noted that in your community there is a need to educate family day care providers about the resources available to them in the public library. In that case, ask to be on the agenda of a meeting of family caregivers. Such meetings are usually sponsored by the licensing agency. Speak to the caregivers themselves to learn what kind of information you can give to them. Plan your program around their specific needs.

Your program may be planned in direct response to a request from a group. If that is the case, communicate with your audience so that the program will be meaningful to them. Librarians are frequently invited to speak before high school child development classes and nursery school parent groups, for example. If you have not been invited, invite yourself, and before preparing your talk, determine the specific needs of the group.

Set goals and objectives for your program. What do you want the participants to get out of your presentation? While your program objectives may be motivational or practical or both, decide in advance what you expect from the participants. You will not be able to determine your methods effectively without clear, well-defined, realistic, goals and objectives. For example, if the objective of your program is to have your participants gain the skills to do preschool story time, you will have to include a reasonable amount of time for practice. On the other hand, if you merely want to motivate the audience to do preschool story time, your program may exclude practice and emphasize demonstration, statistics, and data about the value of reading aloud to preschoolers.

Titles

It is important to give your talk an intriguing title for promotional purposes. The most effective title is usually a catchy phrase to draw the attention of potential participants, followed by a subtitle that describes the program. Examples may be found in the sample outlines in this book. A program for religious educators is entitled "Power of Books: Using Literature in the Religious Education of Young Children." The short, catchy phrase "Power of Books" draws attention; the subtitle describes the program's content more precisely. In some cases a subtitle is not necessary, because the title itself is sufficiently catchy and descriptive to preclude anything further. Alliteration is an effective device to use in a title. "First Books for Your Baby," a title that needs no subtitle is a good example. Don't underestimate the need to assign an attention-grabbing title to your program. It may make the difference between a good turnout and a sparsely attended program. Potential participants may ignore your publicity if they are not attracted by the title; you are also more likely to have publicity run in the media if the title draws the attention of the staff who decide which requests they receive warrant coverage. Be creative, but also be certain that the content of your program is not overshadowed by its title.

Method of Presentation

In the early stages of program planning, it is important to identify your methods. There are many factors to consider.

Your own comfort level is paramount. If you are normally not comfortable talking in front of a group of adults, consider alternatives. Employ, instead, a method that involves the participants in discussion or demonstration or consider doing your program in tandem with a colleague. As an alternative to presenting books from a podium, produce slides of your materials. While slide and talk presentations introduce variety to a program and ensure that a large group can see the books or illustrations to which you refer, they take a great deal of preparation time. Materials must be photographed, film developed, unsatisfactory slides redone, and equipment obtained. Yet slide presentations can be very effective, especially for reluctant speakers.

Also consider the potential size of your group. Demonstration and participation are effective ways of teaching story time skills, but it is not reasonable to expect large groups to learn in this manner. At the same time, lecturing to a handful of people is not effective; if a small audience is expected, a method which involves participants is preferable.

Both the amount of lead time before your program and the amount of preparation time you have to devote are important considerations. Some presentations require a good deal of attention to logistical details—acquisition of additional materials, preparation of the site, and production of giveaways, for example. Keep this in mind when determining how you will present your information.

Date and Time

At this point in the planning of a program, you will need to set the date and time. Communicating with your target audience will help you determine these details. If your audience is to be drawn from many groups, you will want to choose a date and time of day convenient to the majority. Consider that child caregivers are free only on Saturdays and evenings; determine whether most of the parents in your community work during the daytime. If your potential audience is made up of grandparents and other seniors—foster grandparents, for example—daylight hours may be preferable. Be sure you check a calendar thoroughly so that you avoid religious and state holidays. It is impossible to avoid all conflicts, but paying careful attention to holidays and community affairs will help you choose a date and time when your potential audience is most able to attend.

Site and Planning

If you're presenting your program in the library, choose a site conducive to your methods. A large auditorium may be appropriate for a lecture. However, if you're attempting to demonstrate how to do an effective story time, you will want to choose a more intimate setting. Physical comforts can affect the outcome of training and informational programs. Choose your location wisely so that an otherwise effective program is not spoiled by the participants' discomfort. Consider the size of the room and its appropriateness to your objectives; consider acoustics and temperature. If your library does not have an appropriate space, look for another site convenient to you and your audience. As soon as you have chosen a site, date, and time, make the necessary reservations.

If you've been invited to another location, be sure that the facility is suitable for your program; and suggest an alternative site if necessary. You need to be flexible, and you need to consider whether the disadvantages of the site will interfere with the audience's reception of your message.

Once you have set your topic, goals, methods, target audience, location, date, and time, you will need to begin paying attention to the nitty-gritty of preliminary planning. You can use the program planning checklist (fig. 1) to remind yourself of the details months before your actual program. Secure all the necessary approvals from your library administration or from your target audience. Inform those on your staff who will be affected by your presentation and arrange for any necessary adjustments to schedules.

Title of Program _____

Location _____ Time _____

Date _____

Target Audience _____

Goals _____

Methods _____

PRELIMINARY PLANNING

____ Secure necessary approval ____ Arrange for equipment

____ Schedule meeting room ____ Reserve film, filmstrip, etc.

____ Inform staff ____ Obtain necessary funding

____ Adjust schedules and
     arrange for necessary
     staff coverage

PROMOTION

Format

____ Posters ____ Radio public service
                              announcements

____ Flyers

____ Handouts (bookmarks, ____ Television stations and
     bibliographies, etc.)   cable network publicity

____ Newspaper publicity

Contacts

____ Community bulletin boards ____ Posters and flyers outside
                              the library

____ Telephone or letters to
     special agencies ____ Newspaper photographer

____ Television and radio
     interviews

Figure 1. Program Planning Checklist

THREE HOURS BEFORE PROGRAM

Check setup of meeting rooms

_____ Chairs   _____ Pencils   _____ Handouts

_____ Tables   _____ Paper   _____ Refreshments

_____ Equipment   _____ Name tags   _____ Evaluation forms

_____ Materials display   _____ Library card applications

DURING PROGRAM

_____ Take attendance   _____ Collect evaluation forms

_____ Distribute evaluation forms

AFTER PROGRAM

_____ Clean meeting room

_____ Return equipment

_____ Return films, filmstrips, etc.

_____ Pay bills

_____ Record program information for library records

_____ Evaluate program, noting suggestions for improvement and audience reaction

_____ File copies of flyers, publicity, and evaluations

_____ Send thank-you notes to others involved

Figure 1.—Continued

Arrange for staff from another branch or division if necessary. Reserve needed equipment and audiovisual materials. Be sure to preview any film, video, or filmstrip before incorporating it into your program plans.

Materials

It is always a good idea to provide multiple copies of the materials you are speaking about in your program. When you plan your program, determine whether it will be necessary to order materials so that you have a sufficient number of copies for your audience. You may need to seek additional funding to pay for the materials. As an alternative to submitting a supplemental budget to your library, consider other sources of funding, such as grants or corporate assistance.

In addition to ordering multiple copies, you must determine early on what kind of handouts you will supply to your audience. At least prepare a bibliography of the materials you present. A list of titles and authors will facilitate the taking of notes at your program and will eliminate frantic scribbling of titles. It will also serve as a useful reminder of your presentation and the materials you introduced after the program is completed. If participants have the list in front of them, they can use asterisks or short notes to indicate what they've learned about the titles or to highlight ones they've found most interesting. An outline of your talk can be useful to participants. It provides them with paper and facilitates the process of taking notes in much the same way as the bibliography. You may want to save some giveaways for distribution at the end of the program to avoid having participants pay closer attention to your suggested fingerplays or to your name tag patterns than to your talk.

There are many kinds of giveaways to consider, depending on the topic of your program. Resource lists, patterns for name tags, samples of fingerplays and action rhymes are among the handouts often provided at adult programs about children and children's literature. Because program participants may refer to your handouts after your presentation is done, consider including your library's name and the title of your talk on each of your giveaways.

The addition of graphics will improve the appeal of your handouts. If your library does not have a staff artist, you may have to rely on talented coworkers or community artists. Local high school or college students may be willing to work for a nominal fee or for free, if credit for their work is given. Contact art teachers at local schools for recommendations. Visit local art shows to build a resource file of local amateurs or professional graphic artists. Remember to plan your giveaways early enough to allow sufficient time to contact an outside person. When making contacts, state the exact date the graphics are needed and determine an agreed-upon fee if you are able to pay for the work.

It may not be necessary to engage an artist at all. There are many sources for clip art and copyright-free illustrations. Some examples are:

ALA Public Information Office. *Quick Clips: ALA Clip Art III* (Chicago: American Library Association, 1988).

Ludlow, Norman H. *Clip Book Number 10: Shapes, Frames and Borders*. (Rochester, N.Y.: Norman H. Ludlow, 1979).

————. *The Potpourri: Clip Book of Line Artwork*. (Rochester, N.Y.: Norman H. Ludlow, 1979).

Ubinas, Dave. *Clip-Art Book of Cartoon Style Illustrations*. (New York: Arco Publishing, 1983).

Dover Publications, Inc., 30 East 2nd St., Mineola, NY 11501, has a large number of publications listed in their catalog under "Pictorial Archive." The section includes copyright-free art and designs for anyone to use. Catalogs are available upon request.

Dynamic Graphics, Inc., 600 North Forest Park Drive, Peoria, IL 61614-3592, offers *Clipper Creative Art Service*, which includes "Monthly Clip Art," "Clip Bits: The How-to Magazine of Visual Communication" (monthly), "Imagination: Clipper and You—A How-to Introduction to Clipper Creative Art Service," and "Desk Top Art," to be used with Macintosh Desk Top Publishers.

Many librarians use inexpensive rubber stamps to enliven their flyers and booklists. The Kidstamps Company of Ohio is run by two librarians who offer many delightful designs by well-known illustrators, such as Tomie dePaolo, James Marshall, and Trina Schart Hyman. A free catalog is available from Kidstamps, P.O. Box 18699, Cleveland Heights, OH 44118.

Whether you use original art or clip art or decide not to use graphics at all, be sure that your giveaways do not have the appearance of dry and unappealing academic material. Experiment with creative spacing; consider different formats to ensure that people will take the time to peruse your information. For example, arranging a bibliography of preschool literature according to ages or stages of development can make it appear much more readable, as can the elimination of extraneous information. Full bibliographic data is not necessary for a list of materials presented at a program. Catchy headings such as "A Sampler of Good Books for Young Children" or "25 Great Gift Books for Toddlers," will draw attention to a useful list of resources that may otherwise be ignored.

In addition to your handouts, consider other supplies you will want to provide. Paper and pencils for taking notes are a thoughtful courtesy. Name tags allow participants the opportunity to get to know one another. Refreshments are not necessary. But if your program runs more than an hour and a half, a break is desirable, and a refreshment table encourages mingling among participants. Light refreshments available when participants arrive also help to make them feel more at ease, especially if there are many non-library regulars in your audience.

As soon as you have determined the content of your program and the materials you will present in the body of your talk, get started on planning your giveaways. Allow plenty of time to commission or find effective graphics and to devise a format that will be eye-appealing and functional. Consider, also, the necessary lead-time to print or reproduce your handouts. Leaving them to the last minute will only result in a shoddy product. Remember that your giveaways will go home with the participants, and you want them to make a lasting impression.

Hints for Presentation

In the introductions to the seven outlines contained in this book, the originators of the programs have offered hints for presentation that are specific to their program methods, content, and materials. The suggestions were formulated after years of experience addressing adults on a variety of topics and are based on firsthand experiences. You are encouraged to read through the hints in order to glean useful information about seating patterns, time frames, room set-ups, and a variety of other details which contribute to a successful presentation. While some of the hints are specifically intended for particular programs, there are many suggestions which can be applied to any program for adults.

Important Details

If participants have pre-registered, it is a good idea to take attendance. If you have not registered participants or if there are drop-ins in your audience, having them fill out their names and addresses on a sign-up sheet will allow you to invite them personally to any future programs you present.

It is not sufficient just to talk about materials in a program on children's books and activities; it is always important to introduce them to the audience visually as well. You can accomplish this effectively by displaying and holding up the books themselves or by showing slides of illustrations from the books. Even if you are presenting a slide and talk program, it is desirable to mount a book display. Once you have whetted their appetites for your books, your participants will want to see the books themselves. If you are traveling to a site outside the library for your program, it may not be possible to transport all of the books in your presentation. Take as many as you can possibly manage. Once you have sold your audience on the value and beauty of children's books, it is only fair that they have the opportunity to handle and look at them.

Don't limit your displays to books. Depending on the content of your program, other materials may be appropriate. If you're presenting information about story time, you may want to feature records and tapes of children's songs and activities, flannel and story board figures, storytelling aprons, puppets, samples of fold-and-cut stories, and other storytelling aids. Include learning tools, and filmstrips and videos in your display of resources for preschool teachers and day care providers. Regardless of your program topic or your audience, provide library flyers, bookmarks, brochures, and library card applications. Take the opportunity to display as much of the library's printed promotional material as is applicable or related.

It is not enough to pile materials on a table. You must also consider how they look. Your displays should be neat and attractive. Choose the cleanest copies of your books for your table displays; don't use frayed or soiled puppets. Pay close attention to the visual appeal of your display. An inviting display is more likely to be browsed than a messy one.

Although you will want to spend as much time as possible on the content of your presentation, it is wise to allow time at the end of your program for questions and answers and for browsing among your materials. That is not to say that you should not permit questions during your talk; participants should feel free to ask questions at any time during the presentation. However, leaving time at the end for a more formal question and answer period may help the audience feel more comfortable asking questions than they might when they interrupt you in the middle of the program. Many participants feel even more at ease talking to the programmer privately during the browsing time. You can learn a lot during these informal exchanges at the end of a program; participants are often eager to share their own views on your topic or to tell you about their own related successes and failures.

Promotion

After you have devoted the time and energy required to prepare a successful program, you will want to make sure it is well attended and that you will reach those people who will benefit most from your efforts. This chapter's program planning checklist (fig. 1) provides a useful list of promotional ideas about format and contacts. Posters in the library, library publications or calendars of events, flyers and public service announcements in newspapers and on radio and television are typical methods of promoting library programs. Even these standard methods can be utilized in more imaginative and far-reaching ways. Consider inviting a columnist or reporter from the local newspaper to write a feature article on your program. Small community newsletters can provide effective promotion of a program, and their editors are often searching for community news to print. Many of these publications are issued monthly or on an irregular schedule. Consequently, it is necessary to pay particular attention to their deadlines so that your news is featured in the newsletter prior to the program.

Invite a newspaper photographer to the library to take shots of activities related to your program. Photographs of a preschool story time, for example, would be ideal promotion for a program offered for child caregivers on how to read aloud to their children. If the newspaper can provide a photographer for the time of your program, you can use the opportunity to promote your library as well as the program itself. Use every opportunity to get coverage in the media.

Radio and television publicity is particularly effective when you are attempting to draw busy parents and child care providers who may not have the time to read the newspaper. Cable television is a promotional medium growing in popularity. Public access channels, like local community newsletters, are particularly interested in contributors. Introduce yourself to your local cable access channel personnel. They will probably begin contacting you for information to feature once you have established a relationship with them.

In addition to the usual promotional activities cited above, you may want to use the target audiences and suggested contacts for each listed in figure 2. Advertise in newsletters produced by some of the contact agencies and groups. Offer to send flyers to be distributed at meetings or classes and be sure to tell people that they may make additional copies of the flyers. It is a good idea to include a map and directions on your printed publicity when you direct promotional efforts outside the library. Offer to speak briefly at a meeting or class to introduce yourself and to present some details of your program.

Finally, distribute flyers among the contact groups listed in figure 2—doctors' offices, clinics, recreational centers, anywhere your target group might frequent. Many libraries use volunteers for this very worthwhile task. If you can't have publicity delivered personally to the target groups and their contacts, mail them multiple copies of the flyer. An accompanying letter to the leader of the group will add a personal touch.

Above all, get the word out. The more closely you aim your publicity to your target group, the more likely you are to have a good-sized audience of keenly interested participants.

Parents of Young Children; Expectant Parents

Contact: offices of pediatricians, obstetricians, child psychiatrists; La Leche Leagues; Lamaze classes; Mothers of Twins groups; Parents Without Partners groups; well baby clinics; child study associations; church and synagogue groups; local schools offering classes in family life; baby and children's departments in local stores.

Grandparents and Foster Grandparents

Contact: senior citizens' associations; retirement center recreation programs; foster grandparent programs; church and synagogue groups; municipal departments of aging.

Babysitters

Contact: local teen groups; high school classes in child care and family life; Red Cross chapters; 4-H clubs; scout groups; church and synagogue youth groups.

Playground and Playgroup Directors and Staffs

Contact: YMCAs; municipal recreation departments.

Religious Education Instructors

Contact: church and synagogue groups; retailers of religious goods; church-affiliated schools.

Preschool Teachers and Aides

Contact: preschools; Head Start programs; high schools, vocational schools, technical colleges and universities offering classes in child care or programs in early childhood education; local chapters of the Association for the Education of Young Children.

Figure 2. Target audiences and suggested contacts

Evaluation

Before browsing time and before any of your audience leaves, it is important to distribute an evaluation form so that your participants have the opportunity to comment formally on your program. An effective evaluation form will not only elicit reactions to your presentation, but it will also gather information for future programs. Although a long, complicated evaluation document could provide lots of helpful information, it is much more likely that participants will complete a form that is brief and simple.

Child Care Center Staffs

Contact: child care centers; high schools, vocational schools, technical colleges, colleges and universities offering classes in child care
or programs in early childhood education; local chapters of the Association for the Education of Young Children; community health
nurses.

Family Caregivers

Contact: family caregiver associations; municipal and state licensing
agents or agencies; community health nurses; food cooperatives
(many have a newsletter); local chapters of the Association for the
Education of Young Children; high schools, vocational schools, technical colleges, colleges and universities offering classes in child care
or programs in early childhood education.

**Pediatricians, Nurse Practitioners, Pediatric Residents, and Other
Medical Professionals Who Work with Young Children**

Contact: doctors' offices and clinics; well baby clinics; hospital programs for children (call the hospital's public relations department);
medical schools (call the chief pediatrics resident).

**Teachers and Students in Family Life, Child Care, Child Develop-
ment, and Children's Literature Classes**

Contact: high schools, vocational schools, technical colleges, colleges
and universities.

Library Staffs

Contact: public libraries; school libraries; regional and state library associations and media organizations; library schools.

Figure 2.—Continued

A sample form which fits this description is provided in figure 3. If you
choose to develop your own form, you need to do so in the early stages of
program planning. As you develop a form, keep in mind that the purpose
of a participant's evaluation is to assist you in planning future programs and
ultimately to help you improve your service to patrons.

The first question on the sample form, an important component of the
evaluation, deals with promotion. Such a question is the most valid way to
evaluate your promotional efforts. It is not only necessary to determine
what type of publicity attracted the attention of your participants (flyer,

Please help us improve our service by commenting on today's program.

1. How did you learn about this program?
   Flyer—Where did you see it? _____
   Poster—Where did you see it? _____
   Newspaper _____ Radio _____ School _____ Another Person _____
   Other—Please explain _____

2. Was this program useful to you? Useful _____ Not useful _____

3. What did you find the most helpful? _____
   _____

4. How could the program be improved? _____
   _____

5. Would you be interested in attending more library-sponsored programs? Yes _____ No _____

6. Suggestions for programs you would like to see offered:
   _____
   _____

7. What day of the week would be best for another program?
   _____ What time of day? _____

8. Additional comments: _____
   _____
   _____
   _____

Thank you!

Figure 3. Participant's Evaluation of Library Program

poster, or public service announcement, for example), but also to identify where they saw or heard the notice of your program. If no one came to your program as a result of announcements in a particular newspaper, you will be able to eliminate that publication from future publicity distributions. If a medium attracted an unusually large number of people, you will want to target and expand that coverage. The essential point is to use the information participants give you so that your future promotional efforts are as effective as possible.

The next part of the evaluation form is concerned with the program content and presentation. It is helpful to ask your participants to rate the program content on a numerical scale. Simplicity is preferable; a five point scale provides enough information. The rating of a program from unsatisfactory to excellent provides sufficient input for a programmer to determine how well a presentation was received. Narrative comments on the content and presentation of the program are also useful. They afford the participant the opportunity to provide you with information you can use to revise future programs. The questions "What did you find most helpful?" and "How could the program be improved?" which appear on the sample form, elicit useful comments for programmers.

The remainder of the sample evaluation form requests other information for planning future programs—suggestions for other topics and preferred dates and times. The evaluation closes with a space for additional comments.

Only a very small percentage of the people in attendance at a program will actually complete an evaluation form without prodding. Don't let this discourage you from seeking participant input. A gentle reminder at the opening of the program and again at the close, as well as a clearly marked collection point near the exit of the room, will help ensure a respectable return.

Once you have received the participants' evaluations, you will need to compile them and include the information in your own evaluation of the program. Even if your library does not require a formal evaluation, it is important for you to determine the strengths and weaknesses of the presentation for yourself. Note suggestions for improvement and highlight what went especially well. If possible, share your evaluation with your co-workers. They can benefit from your experience, and you may encourage them to program for adults as well.

Conclusion

Before you file away all the notes and documents from your program, attend to follow-up details. Record all necessary information for your library records—attendance and numbers of books checked out, for example. Pay any outstanding bills. Send thank-you notes to others involved—the newspaper photographer who recorded your program on film, the public health nurse who distributed your flyers, the circulation department staff who rushed to check out materials to your audience as the library was closing. Include anyone who may have contributed to the success of your program. They all need to know that you appreciate their assistance and support.

Attention to the details of program planning outlined in the checklist (fig. 1) will not ensure a flawless program. However, it will guard against failure and contribute to success even when children's librarians are programming for adults for the first time.

Seven Library Programs

1. First Books for Your Baby

CAROLINE FELLER BAUER

INTENDED AUDIENCE: Expectant parents

LENGTH: Forty minutes, plus time to examine books

SUMMARY OF PROGRAM: This lecture and demonstration introduces new and expectant parents to the joys and delights of children's literature. The objective is simply to get the audience excited about children's books. The lecture does not attempt to give reasons why one should read to children; it does attempt to overwhelm the audience with the wonder of children's books.

HINTS FOR PLANNING AND PRESENTATION: This is your big chance to introduce adults to a new, lasting and useful hobby. The program is not just for first-time parents; invite everyone! But aim your publicity at expectant parents. Take advantage of their enthusiasm and get them interested in books before they are immersed in all the work of parenting. If you can do this, they will continue to explore books for the fun of it as well as for the edification of their children. Be sure to invite dads as well as moms, and include the men in your talk. Keep the group small enough so that everyone can see the pictures in the books you show.

Present your talk in an informal, relaxed manner so your audience will not be afraid to make comments or ask questions.

Exhibit a variety of the newest picture books to show that there is a book for every taste, no matter how conservative or bizarre! Distribute an annotated bibliography to match your book display. I like to develop a new list every year to showcase my favorite new titles.

I. INTRODUCTION

A. Stress the excitement and pleasure in store for your audience as they begin to learn about the wonderful world of children's books.

B. Briefly discuss the tremendous increase in the publication of children's books, especially books for babies and toddlers in the past several years.

C. Point out that bookstores simply do not have the space to display all the books published for young children; supermarkets and toy stores have an even smaller selection. The public library offers the best access to a wide variety of children's books. Encourage your audience to think of children's librarians as subject specialists who can offer them valuable guidance.

II. A LOOK AT THE VARIETY OF "BABY BOOKS" AVAILABLE TODAY

A. Show *Pat the Bunny*.[1] One of the most satisfying baby books was published many years ago. Now considered a classic, Dorothy Kunhardt's *Pat the Bunny* introduces baby to the simple pleasures of playing peek-a-boo, waving good-bye, feeling Daddy's scratchy beard, and patting a soft bunny.

B. Show a selection of *object identification* books. A major parent obsession is teaching a child to communicate. When we visit a foreign country we're always a bit peeved that small children are speaking Chinese or French fluently when we can't even say "thank you." The truth is that it took those children two or three years to learn their native language. It will take your child that long to speak English. You can help by speaking to your child as much as possible and by using the *look say* method with books. There are many children's books that show an object common to the child's world and give the word for that object next to it or underneath it. You'll find words like house, dog, chair. If you live in a climate like Hawaii's, you'll probably be surprised to find the word mittens, but keep in mind that mittens is a word, too.

C. Show examples of cloth and board books. When babies are brand new, they will not be able to hold a book or turn the pages. You, your spouse, Grandma, or Uncle Harry will do that. But as soon as children can reach out they'll grab for the book. This is the time to try board books or cloth books. These books are made for tough handling, grabbing, and biting. A child needs to learn how to grasp a page and turn it, but you cannot expect this to happen for many months.

D. Show sets of books by major authors and illustrators, such as Jan Ormerod, Anne Rockwell, Rosemary Wells, and Peter Spier. These are books written and offered individually but also as part of a group. You'll soon learn the authors' and illustrators' names, and

1. Dorothy Kunhardt, *Pat the Bunny* (Racine, Wis.: Western Publishing Co., 1942).

you'll enjoy the books they've produced for older children as your child grows.

III. ALTERNATIVE INTRODUCTIONS TO THE WORLD OF PAPER AND PRINT

    A. Show a variety of magazines with big pictures. Include nature magazines, food magazines, and special magazines like *Life*. Show several full-color mail order catalogs and some illustrated greeting cards. You don't always need a bound book to introduce children to paper and print. These non-book materials can introduce your baby to the world of paper and print as well as any book. You don't need an author's text to go with the pictures. Simply talk to your baby about what is in the pictures.

    B. Show a roll of wax paper; unroll it. One of my favorite gifts for a six-month old is a roll of waxed paper. The child can learn about paper—by crinkling, pulling or smashing it—without destroying a book.

IV. READING ALOUD

    A. Encourage parents to read to their children as often as possible— even several times a day. Establish a tradition of the "lunch book" or the "nap book" as well as the "bedtime" book.

    B. Suggest that parents involve the whole family—mom, dad, siblings, and even the family dog—in share-a-book time.

    C. Emphasize that parents should not feel that they have to share a different book every time they read to their children. Young children adore repetition.

V. WHERE TO GO FROM HERE

    A. Distribute an annotated bibliography designed to show the vast range of picture books. Explain that this is a small sampling of the many delightful books published for young children. Over 4,000 children's books are published each year.

    B. Booktalk a few of your favorite new picture books for older children, emphasizing the fantastic variety of books to choose from as children grow and become avid listeners.

    C. Once again, encourage your audience to look for these and other titles at the public library. Leave them with the thought that there is a book for every child and for every adult who wants to share.

2. Raising Reading Children

MARALITA L. FREENY

INTENDED AUDIENCE: Parents of preschoolers

LENGTH: One and a half hours

SUMMARY OF PROGRAM: This program was designed to encourage parents to read to their children beginning in infancy and to provide suggestions for types of books and specific titles that can be read during different stages of development, from birth to five years. In order to accomplish the first of these purposes, the presentation outlines the beneficial effects of reading aloud on a child's reading readiness and language development. It is not, however, the intention of the presentation to encourage the teaching of reading to preschoolers.

The second portion of the program matches types of picture books and specific, well-chosen favorite titles to the different stages of development.

HINTS FOR PLANNING AND PRESENTATION: The first thirty minutes of the program are devoted to informal lecturing on the benefits of reading aloud. The facts and much of the philosophy presented in the program are extracted from the writings of Dorothy Butler's *Babies Need Books*[1] and the National Council of Teachers of English publication *Raising Readers: A Guide to Sharing Literature with Young Children*.[2] It is vital to give specific credit to these authors and their two books in the introduction and throughout the talk.

Approximately an hour is necessary to introduce the actual picture books to the audience. It will be helpful to distribute a list of the titles and authors in order to facilitate taking notes on the books. This portion of the program is based largely on the book *Raising Readers*. I have substituted my own favorite books for those cited by the authors and have researched other child development texts for ideas on how to present the different

---

1. Dorothy Butler, *Babies Need Books* (New York: Atheneum, 1980).
2. National Council of Teachers of English, *Raising Readers: A Guide to Sharing Literature with Young Children* (New York: Walker, 1980).

stages of development. Presenters using this sample outline should also use their own favorites so that their enthusiasm for children's literature becomes apparent to the audience.

Librarians who lack enthusiasm for picture books or for the concepts outlined should refrain from making the presentation.

I have adapted this talk for various audiences. While I originally planned it as a public library program for parents, I have used it, with little alteration, for day care center parents and teachers and as in-service training for children's librarians. Adding a section on how to read to babies and concluding at the child's 18-month developmental stage, I have presented this talk at a professional association workshop titling it "Infant Literature." By beginning at the 3-year-old developmental stage and by adjusting the first portion of the talk slightly, taking out the emphasis on babies, I have also used it with nursery school parent groups. Other variations are possible, including some that use material from this publication.

I. INTRODUCTION

A. Present purpose of the program.
1. To encourage parents to read to preschoolers beginning when children are in infancy.
2. To emphasize and explain the importance of reading aloud.
3. To guide parents toward good books that match the different developmental stages of their children.

B. Discuss how I became interested in this topic.
1. My experience as a parent was as important as my numerous years as a children's librarian. Possibly it was more important. It wasn't until my husband began reading to our infant son that I realized the positive effect that reading aloud has on a baby.
2. Years of reading to my two children have reinforced that realization and heightened my respect for children's capabilities with regard to books and language.

C. Discuss how my experience with reading aloud led me to the writings of Dorothy Butler and the National Council of Teachers of English on whose research and philosophies this talk is based.
1. Dorothy Butler's *Babies Need Books* provided both the inspiration and many of the facts presented throughout the talk.
2. *Raising Readers*, written by the National Council of Teachers of English, Committee on Literature in the Elementary Language Arts, headed by Linda Lamme, provided the basis for the types of literature appropriate to each stage.

II. WHY BOTHER TO READ

    A. Fifty percent of human intellectual development takes place between birth and four years of age. Therefore, what you do during the earliest years of a child's life truly makes a difference.

    B. Reading aloud establishes a favorable climate for learning.

    C. Reading aloud establishes reading as an important activity.

        1. The process of learning to read already occupies a prominent place in our society. Reading as a pleasurable activity, on the other hand, is ignored. Yet, it is only through their desire to read that children learn how to read successfully.

        2. Toys sell well in our world today; unfortunately, books do not share the same popularity.

    D. Reading aloud provides an opportunity for the reader and the child to cuddle and to enjoy a warm physical relationship.

    E. Reading can bridge gaps among generations. A good children's book is as enjoyable to adults as it is to children.

    F. Reading aloud is an excellent means to facilitate problem solving by establishing a trusting relationship between parent and child.

III. READING ALOUD VERSUS TEACHING READING

    A. This talk is not intented to encourage parents to teach their children to read at an early age, although children involved with reading from babyhood often do learn to read early.

    B. Introduce books for pleasure even though learning is the outcome of having been read to on a regular basis.

    C. Even if they don't learn to read before they go to school, children read to regularly tend to be more confident about their ability to learn to read and, therefore, learn more easily when formal instruction begins. Children comfortable with books and reading are more successful in learning to read than children unfamiliar with books.

IV. READING ALOUD AND ITS EFFECTS ON READING READINESS

    A. Babies attain many readiness skills in their first year.

        1. Listening.

        2. Turning pages.

        3. Determining top of page from bottom.

        4. Discriminating among objects on a page.

        5. Discovering that pictures have meaning.

B. Older children attain more sophisticated reading readiness skills.

1. Visual and auditory discrimination, such as determining the sounds of letters and how the printed letters look.

2. Reading has consistent rules. For example, English is read from left to right.

3. There is a relationship between the printed word and spoken language.

V. READING ALOUD AND LANGUAGE DEVELOPMENT

A. Researchers and educators agree that language is the best tool of learning.

B. In order to learn to express themselves at an early age and in a more fluent manner, children need to be exposed to complex speech patterns. Speaking to children in rich, fluent language will probably enrich their language development.

C. It is not necessary to use simple sentence structure and vocabulary in direct conversations with small children. Reading provides the richness and variety of language children need to hear. There is no easier way to present good, fluent language than through a good, well-written book.

VI. PROVIDING GOOD LITERATURE

A. The public library is an excellent place to find good books to read to babies, toddlers, and preschoolers. Most public libraries have staff members trained to work with children. Regular visits to the library to borrow books should be scheduled. Although children love the repetition of reading and rereading their favorite books, they also need the variety available at the library.

B. Having books around the house is important. Having personal collections of books in the home shows that you think reading and books are important. Purchase your child's favorites from your local book retailer or at your public library's book sales. The budget-conscious parent can find many high-quality picture books available in paperback.

VII. BOOKS TO MATCH CHILDREN'S DEVELOPMENTAL STAGES

A. Infancy. Emphasize that developmental stages vary from child to child. Publishers have been slow to realize that babies constitute an audience for books. For example, the excellent Brimax series of books is appropriate for infants, but according to the covers of the books, its publisher is promoting it for two- to four-year-olds.

1. Developing a sense of hearing.

   In the earliest months, read anything—newspapers, your favorite magazines, a professional journal.

   In the earliest months, the sound of a voice is more important than the sense of what is being read. Therefore, Mother Goose books are among the best first books for babies. The rhymes are melodic and easily memorized, and they can be used anywhere by parents who want to amuse their children. Later, as children learn to talk, they will be able to memorize and recite the rhymes easily, giving themselves a sense of accomplishment. Raymond Briggs' *Mother Goose Treasury* is a good collection of rhymes and a good first book.

   Song books, poetry, and the so-called sound or noise books are also appropriate for infants. *Hush Little Baby*, *Animal Noises*, and *Crash! Bang! Boom!* present interesting songs and sounds for babies.

   Sharon, Lois and Bram's Mother Goose includes both rhymes and songs and makes an excellent gift for a new baby.

2. Developing a sense of touch.

   Board books lend themselves to use by babies. They are nearly indestructible. Babies can pull or chew on them. Good choices among the many board books available are *Animal ABC*, *Are There Hippos on the Farm?*, and *All Fall Down*.

   Texture or *touch and feel* books are appropriate when children are developing their sense of touch. *Pat the Bunny*, now a classic, provides a variety of textures for baby to experience.

3. Developing clearer vision when the eyes begin to focus.

   Books with large, clear, uncluttered illustrations in bright, primary colors provide the best visual experience when baby's eyes first begin to focus. Naming books, alphabet books, and color and number books, such as *Brian Wildsmith's ABC* and *I Spy*, are examples.

4. Identifying objects.

   In their earliest experiences with books, children especially delight in finding objects on a page. *Baby's Catalogue* is a naming book that is appropriate.

   Number, alphabet, and color books also lend themselves to point and name activities with a parent. *Colors* by Pienkowski and Oxenbury's *Numbers of Things* are good choices to use.

5. Naming objects.

   In order to enhance language development, use the books

cited earlier, but instead of having the child point to the object and the parent name it, the parent should point and have the child do the naming. *The Great Big Animal Book*, *Early Words*, and *Mr. Gumpy's Outing* are illustrated with pictures of items children can easily learn to identify.

B. Toddler years. The books you use during these years will depend on whether or not you read to the child during her infancy. It is not necessary to limit books to those with vocabularies within the immediate experience of the child.

   1. Developing manual dexterity.

      Use books that are small, "little books for little hands." Small board books, such as *You Do It Too, Muppets in My Neighborhood*, and *Max's New Suit*, are appropriate for toddlers to handle even without supervision.

      Little books with paper pages, such as *Young Joe* and *The Rabbit*, are also easily handled by toddlers, but adults must supervise their use more closely.

   2. More advanced language usage.

      More complicated alphabet, naming, sound, and number books can be used to enhance the toddler's rapidly developing language. Try *Wild Animals* and *A-B-Cing*.

      Descriptive books, such as *My Day on the Farm, Our Cat Flossie*, and *A Winter Day*, are excellent books to use for language development while a child's attention span is too short to use picture stories effectively.

   3. Negativism.

      Books which ask questions, especially when the appropriate answers are negative, are ideal for the stage when the toddler's favorite word is "no."

      How Do I Put It On? and *Where's Spot?* are two favorite books with questions answered in the negative.

   4. Sense of accomplishment.

      Flap books, such as *Dear Zoo* and the Spot series, provide a sense of accomplishment to toddlers, who quickly learn how and when to lift the flap.

      When children can independently know when to turn the page, they feel a sense of accomplishment. Simple stories are good to use as is a good collection of Mother Goose rhymes, for example, *Tomie dePaola's Mother Goose*.

   5. Learning simple concepts, such as numbers, letters, colors, and days of the week.

Simple concepts can be taught through a good book. *Freight Train, Brown Bear, Brown Bear, What Do You See?*, and *Rain* introduce colors within a lively and appealing context.

Good books to use to teach counting and number recognition are *One Hunter* and *Who's Counting?*

6. Increased attention spans.

Simple descriptive books can be followed by short, simple stories with believable situations. The story is all important; the text must be good. Look for books by Eve Rice, Pat Hutchins, Ann Jonas, and Eric Carle. *Benny Bakes a Cake* by Rice, *Titch* by Hutchins, *Two Bear Cubs* by Jonas, and *The Very Hungry Caterpillar* by Carle are among my favorites.

It's okay for animals to act like children in these stories. *Wide-Awake Timothy* is a good example of a short, simple story in which an animal, in this case a koala bear, is very childlike.

C. Three-year-olds. I can't emphasize enough how important it is to remember that children develop at different rates. Some three-year-olds will be ready for the books listed in this section; some will have devoured them during their toddler years. The following are merely loose guidelines to help you in your selections.

1. Increased interest in the use of words.

Poetry provides richness of language and rhythm which enhances a child's interest in language. *Poems to Read to the Very Young, Read-Aloud Rhymes for the Very Young,* and *Every Time I Climb a Tree* are collections that are personal favorites of mine. "Mary Had a Little Lamb" and "Three Little Kittens" are examples of single rhymes that are often illustrated and published as whole books.

Nonsense books present new words to youngsters who are becoming really interested in language. These same books also demonstrate rhythm and cadence. In addition to books by the well-known Dr. Seuss, *Jamberry* is a good choice.

The repetition in cumulative stories also provides a rich experience for the preschooler who has an increased interest in language. Good cumulative stories are *Napping House, Lisa Cannot Sleep,* and *The Cake That Mack Ate.*

2. Growing independence and sense of accomplishment.

Books that allow the child to participate in the telling are ideal for three-year-olds. Children respond to the hidden pictures and shapes in *Each Peach Pear Plum* and *It Looked like Spilt Milk. The Most Amazing Hide-and-Seek Alphabet Book* is an unusually fine tab book which also invites participation by the child.

Singing is another way to involve children in books. Songs illustrated and published as whole books can be used to accomplish this. *Wheels on the Bus, Mary Wore Her Red Dress, The Lady with the Alligator Purse,* and *The Cat Goes Fiddle-i-fee* are always popular.

3. Development of self-esteem.

As children develop their personalities and accept themselves, they will respond to books with characters with whom they can identify.

Ezra Jack Keats, Shirley Hughes, and Rosemary Wells are some good authors to use. Sample books by these authors are *Whistle for Willie, Alfie's Feet,* and *Noisy Nora.* While Wells' characters are usually animals, children will have no trouble identifying with them.

4. Comfort with familiar things.

Preschoolers are curious about the world around them, but they are most comfortable with the familiar. Read books about their everyday life, about their pets, their toys, their experiences in the community. Try *Harry the Dirty Dog* or *Kitten up a Tree,* excellent stories about pets; or try *My Barber* and *The Supermarket* by Anne and Harlow Rockwell, who have written about a variety of everyday experiences.

5. Advanced concept-learning.

Books can encourage a child's understanding of concepts. Shapes, spatial relationships, and time are within the grasp of a three-year-old.

Look Around, Where Is My Friend?, and *Blue Sea* introduce shapes, spatial relationships, and contrasting sizes respectively.

6. Developing imagination.

Read books that appeal to the child's imagination. Books that personify animals, toys, and other things are well-liked by three-year-olds.

Look for books by Don Freeman; his *Corduroy and Dandelion* are sure-fire hits.

Mike Mulligan and His Steam Shovel, in which a steam shovel has a personality, has become a classic.

7. Need for parental love and security.

Mood books, or books that help children settle down are appropriate for this age. Books like *Ten, Nine, Eight, Whose*

Mouse Are You?, *The Moon Came Too*, and *Goodnight, Moon* are perfect for sharing at nap time or bedtime.

Read books that reflect parental love, for instance *On Mother's Lap* and *Claude and Pepper*.

D. Four- and five-year-olds.

    1. Desire for fairness.

Older preschoolers have a strong feeling about what is and isn't fair. They like and want poetic justice of the kind that is present in *The Tale of Peter Rabbit*. They also like happy endings in books in which a character has been in danger. *Gunniwolf* and *Swimmy* are prime examples.

Beast fairy tales are appropriate at this stage. Pre-read fairy tales so that you are not disappointed with unfamiliar variations. For example, in some versions of "The Three Little Pigs," the pigs are eaten by the wolf; in others, all three escape unharmed. Determine which version you have before reading it aloud to the child. Many versions of traditional fairy tales are nicely illustrated. Paul Galdone's *The Three Bears* comes to mind, as does *Red Riding Hood* by James Marshall.

Modern non-traditional fairy tales are popular with four- and five-year-olds. *The Straw Maid* and *The Little Girl and the Big Bear* are personal favorites of my family.

    2. Curiosity about the world at large.

Older preschoolers become interested in the world outside their own everyday experiences. They yearn to find out about science, religion, history, famous people, other lands, and more. Factual picture books are now in plentiful supply on this level. Gail Gibbons is a prolific author to remember. Her non-fiction books are brief, precise, and quite interesting. *Boat Book* is just one example.

The world of science is widely represented in preschool books. *Snakes*, *In My Garden*, and *The Sky Is Full of Stars* are just three examples of the many excellent books available.

To introduce history, you can read stories based on truth as well as traditional nonfiction books. *Watch the Stars Come Out* is an appealing historical picture story; *The Story of the Statue of Liberty* is an example of a factual historical picture book.

    3. Advanced verbal skills.

Wordless books encourage children to be creative and expressive by allowing them to tell stories in their own words. *Apples* and *Creepy Castle* are two such wordless picture books.

Panorama books, such as those made popular by Richard

Scarry, provide detailed illustrations just waiting for children with advanced verbal skills to describe. *Richard Scarry's Best Word Book Ever* is one of the author's best.

4. Increased attention span.

There is less need for illustrations in the stories you share with four- and five-year-olds. You will now be able to read the many excellent, longer picture book stories, especially folk stories. Try *Tikki Tikki Tembo* and *Snow White and the Seven Dwarfs.*

Collections of stories are suitable for this age. Rockwell's *Three Bears and Fifteen Other Stories* is a good choice as is *Tomie dePaola's Favorite Nursery Tales.*

5. Adventurous nature.

Four- and five-year-olds love adventure and suspense in their books; many children this age enjoy being scared.

Adventure books to read are *Jumanji; Crictor; Pig Pig Grows Up,* and *May We Sleep Here Tonight?*

6. Advanced sense of humor.

Children at this stage begin to understand the humor in many situations. Jack Kent writes wonderfully funny books for this age. *Round Robin* and *The Once-upon-a-Time Dragon* are examples of his best work.

You will laugh along with your child when you read *Jim and the Beanstalk* and *Pickle Things.*

VIII. WRAP-UP

A. Question and answer period.

B. Browsing through books.

C. Tour of the library.

A Booklist

Ahlberg, Janet, and Allan Ahlberg. *Baby's Catalogue.* Little, 1983.
———. *Each Peach Pear Plum.* Viking, 1979.
Aliki, illus. *Hush Little Baby: A Folk Lullaby.* Prentice-Hall, 1968.
Bang, Molly. *Ten, Nine, Eight.* Greenwillow, 1983.
Beckman, Kaj. *Lisa Cannot Sleep.* Watts, 1969.
Beller, Janet. *A-B-Cing: An Action Alphabet.* Crown, 1985.
Branley, Franklyn M. *The Sky Is Full of Stars.* Illus. by Felicia Bond. Harper, 1983.

Briggs, Raymond. *Jim and the Beanstalk*. Putnam, 1980.

————, illus. *Mother Goose Treasury*. Putnam, 1966.

Brown, Marc. *Pickle Things*. Parents, 1980.

Brown, Margaret Wise. *Goodnight, Moon*. Illus. by Clement Hurd. Harper, 1949.

Brown, Ruth. *Our Cat Flossie*. Dutton, 1986.

Burningham, John. *Mr. Gumpy's Outing*. Holt, 1971.

————. *The Rabbit*. Harper, 1975.

Burton, Virginia Lee. *Mike Mulligan and His Steam Shovel*. Houghton Mifflin, 1939.

Campbell, Rod. *Dear Zoo*. Macmillan, 1984.

Carle, Eric. *The Very Hungry Caterpillar*. Putnam, 1981.

Carlstrom, Nancy. *The Moon Came Too*. Illus. by Stella Ormai. Macmillan, 1987.

Crews, Donald. *Freight Train*. Greenwillow, 1978.

Crowther, Robert. *The Most Amazing Hide-and-Seek Alphabet Book*. Viking, 1978.

Degen, Bruce. *Jamberry*. Harper, 1983.

dePaola, Tomie. *Tomie dePaola's Favorite Nursery Tales*. Putnam, 1986.

————, illus. *Tomie dePaola's Mother Goose*. Putnam, 1985.

Fisher, Leonard Everett. *Look Around! A Book about Shapes*. Viking, 1987.

Florian, Douglas. *A Winter Day*. Greenwillow, 1987.

Freeman, Don. *Corduroy*. Viking, 1968.

————. *Dandelion*. Viking, 1964.

Gackenback, Dick. *Claude and Pepper*. Houghton Mifflin, 1976.

Galdone, Joanna. *The Little Girl and the Big Bear*. Houghton Mifflin, 1980.

Galdone, Paul. *The Cat Goes Fiddle-i-fee*. Ticknor and Fields, 1985.

————. *The Three Bears*. Houghton Mifflin, 1972.

Galdone, Paul, illus. *Three Little Kittens*. Ticknor and Fields, 1986.

Gibbons, Gail. *Boat Book*. Holiday, 1983.

Goodall, John S. *Creepy Castle*. Atheneum, 1975.

Grimm, Jakob. *Snow White and the Seven Dwarfs*. Illus. by Nancy Burkert. Farrar, 1972.

Hale, Sara Josepha. *Mary Had a Little Lamb*. Illus. by Tomie dePaola. Holiday, 1984.

Harper, Wilhelmena. *Gunniwolf*. Illus. by William Wiesner. Dutton, 1967.

Hill, Eric. *Where's Spot?* Putnam, 1987.

Hogrogian, Nonny. *Apples*. Macmillan, 1972.

Hughes, Shirley. *Alfie's Feet*. Lothrop, 1983.

Hutchins, Pat. *One Hunter*. Greenwillow, 1982.

————. *Titch*. Macmillan, 1971.

Jonas, Ann. *Two Bear Cubs*. Greenwillow, 1982.

Kalan, Robert. *Blue Sea*. Illus. by Donald Crews. Greenwillow, 1979.

————. *Rain*. Illus. by Donald Crews. Greenwillow, 1978.

Kanao, Keiki. *Kitten up a Tree*. Knopf, 1987.

Keats, Ezra Jack. *Whistle for Willie*. Viking, 1964.

Kent, Jack. *The Once-upon-a-Time Dragon*. Harcourt, 1982.

————. *Round Robin*. Prentice-Hall, 1982.

Kessler, Ethel, and Len Kessler. *Are There Hippos on the Farm?* Simon and Schuster, 1987.

Kilroy, Sally. *Animal Noises*. Four Winds, 1983.

Koide, Tan. *May We Sleep Here Tonight?* Macmillan, 1983.

Kraus, Robert. *Whose Mouse Are You?* Illus. by José Aruego. Macmillan, 1970.

Kunhardt, Dorothy. *Pat the Bunny*. Western, 1942.

Levinson, Riki. *Watch the Stars Come Out*. Illus. by Dianne Goode. Dutton, 1985.

Lionni, Leo. *Swimmy*. Pantheon, 1966.

Lobel, Anita. *The Straw Maid*. Greenwillow, 1983.

McCord, David. *Every Time I Climb a Tree*. Ed. by Marc Simont. Little, 1967.

McPhail, David. *Pig Pig Grows Up*. Dutton, 1980.

Maestro, Betsy. *The Story of the Statue of Liberty*. Lothrop, 1986.

————. *Where Is My Friend?* Illus. by Giulio Maestro. Crown, 1976.

Marshall, James. *Red Riding Hood*. Dial, 1987.

Martin, Bill, Jr. *Brown Bear, Brown Bear, What Do You See?* Illus. by Eric Carle. Holt, 1983.

Mosel, Arlene. *Tikki Tikki Tembo*. Illus. by Blair Lent. Holt, 1968.

Nakatani, Chiyoko. *My Day on the Farm*. Crowell, 1976.

Oechsli, Helen, and Kelly Oechsli. *In My Garden*. Macmillan, 1985.

Ogle, Lucille. *I Spy: A Picture Book of Objects*. American Heritage, 1970.

Ormerod, Jan. *Young Joe*. Lothrop, 1985.

Oxenbury, Helen. *All Fall Down*. Macmillan, 1987.

————. *Numbers of Things*. Watts, 1968.

Peek, Merle. *Mary Wore Her Red Dress*. Ticknor and Fields, 1985.

Petty, Kate. *Snakes*. Illus. by Alan Baker. Watts, 1985.

Pienkowski, Jan. *Colors*. Simon and Schuster, 1981.

Poems to Read to the Very Young. Ed. by Frank Josette. Illus. by Dagmar Wilson. Random, 1982.

Potter, Beatrix. *The Tale of Peter Rabbit*. Warne, 1987.

Raffi. *Wheels on the Bus*. Illus. by Sylvie K. Wickstrom. Crown, 1988.

Read-Aloud Rhymes for the Very Young. Ed. by Jack Prelutsky. Illus. by Marc Brown. Knopf, 1986.

Rice, Eve. *Benny Bakes a Cake*. Greenwillow, 1981.

Robart, Rose. *The Cake That Mack Ate.* Illus. by Maryann Kovalski. Little, 1987.

Rockwell, Anne F. *Three Bears and Fifteen Other Stories.* Harper, 1975.

————, and Harlow Rockwell. *My Barber.* Macmillan, 1981.

————. *The Supermarket.* Macmillan, 1979.

Rojankovsky, Feodor. *Great Big Animal Book.* Golden, 1950.

Scarry, Richard. *Early Words.* Random House, 1976.

————. *Richard Scarry's Best Word Book Ever.* Western, 1963.

Scott, Ann Herbert. *On Mother's Lap.* Illus. by Glo Coolson. McGraw, 1972.

Sesame Street. *Muppets in My Neighborhood.* Random, 1977.

Sharon, Lois, and Bram. *Sharon, Lois and Bram's Mother Goose.* Atlantic Monthly Pr., 1986.

Shaw, Charles G. *It Looked like Spilt Milk.* Harper, 1988.

Spier, Peter. *Crash! Bang! Boom!* Doubleday, 1972.

Tafuri, Nancy. *Who's Counting?* Greenwillow, 1986.

Ungerer, Tomi. *Crictor.* Harper, 1958.

Van Allsburg, Chris. *Jumanji.* Houghton Mifflin, 1981.

Wakefield, Joyce. *Wide-Awake Timothy.* Childrens Pr., 1981.

Watanabe, Shigeo. *How Do I Put It On?* Putnam, 1980.

Wells, Rosemary. *Max's New Suit.* Dial, 1979.

————. *Noisy Nora.* Dial, 1973.

Westcott, Nadine Bernard. *The Lady with the Alligator Purse.* Little, 1988.

Wildsmith, Brian. *ABC.* Watts, 1962.

————. *Wild Animals.* Oxford University, 1976.

Woods, Audrey. *Napping House.* Illus. by Don Woods. Harcourt, 1984.

Wynne, Patricia. *Animal ABC.* Random, 1977.

Zion, Gene. *Harry the Dirty Dog.* Harper, 1956.

Resources for Adults

Boegehold, Betty D. *Getting Ready to Read.* Ballantine, 1984.

Presents pre-reading preparation that parents can practice with their children. Boegeold stresses that getting children ready to read is more important than the actual teaching of reading itself, and emphasizes the importance of giving children a rich reading background from babyhood.

Butler, Dorothy. *Babies Need Books.* Atheneum, 1985.

Dorothy Butler builds a strong case for parents to begin reading to children during infancy. She also provides advice on the ways, means, and materials.

————. *Reading Begins at Home: Preparing Children for Reading before They Go to School.* Heinemann Educational Books, 1982.

Basic and highly practical advice is given to parents on how to introduce reading readiness skills to their children.

Carlson, Ann D. *Early Childhood Literature Sharing Programs in Libraries.* Library Professional Publications, 1985.

Extensive research in child development literature is the basis of Carlson's outline of childhood growth patterns. Carlson, a librarian, charts children's interests and abilities from birth to thirty-six months and matches them with related activities.

Cascardi, Andrea E. *Good Books to Grow On: A Guide to Building Your Child's Library from Birth to Age Five.* Warner Books, 1985.

This handbook combines the advice found in many parenting bibles and books about children and reading.

Cianciolo, Patricia Jean. *Picture Books for Children.* American Library Association, 1981.

In addition to an annotated list of outstanding picture books, Cianciolo's book includes an informative introduction that examines and describes current trends and explores the values and uses of picture books and criteria for evaluating them.

Cohen, Dorothy H. *The Learning Child.* Vintage Books, 1972.

How to prepare children for learning to read is one of the aspects of childhood learning covered in this guide written by a teacher of child development at the famous Bank Street College.

Cooperman, Paul. *Taking Books to Heart: How to Develop a Love of Reading in Your Child.* Addison-Wesley, 1986.

Laying the foundation for a child's future reading success is the goal of Cooperman's Family Reading Program for Pre-School Children, presented in this guide. The techniques outlined will make reading aloud easy, fun, and of maximum benefit to the child.

Hearne, Betsy. *Choosing Books for Children: A Commonsense Guide.* Delacorte, 1981.

Chapters in this practical guide are devoted to the selection of children's books from preschool picture stories to young adult fiction. The annotated lists offer good starting points for anyone interested in exploring books for youngsters.

Kaye, Peggy. *Games for Reading: Playful Ways to Help Your Child Read.* Pantheon Books, 1984.

More than seventy easy-to-follow games that require little or no preparation are presented for the purpose of encouraging reading.

Larrick, Nancy. *A Parent's Guide to Children's Reading.* Bantam, 1982.

In this fifth edition of her work, children's book authority Nancy Larrick guides parents toward helping their children develop their reading skills as well as a taste for reading. She shows how to make reading stimulating for children of all ages.

Lipson, Eden Ross. *The New York Times Parent's Guide to the Best Books for Children*. Times Books, 1988.

Parents will recognize many of their old favorites among the picture books and story books featured in this guide. Dozens of special indexes make it easy to match the right book to the right child.

McMullan, Kate Hall. *How to Choose Good Books for Kids*. Addison-Wesley, 1984.

McMullan presents guidelines for selecting books to match the various developmental stages from birth to age eleven. She includes a list of books, illustrated with original drawings from the selections.

National Council of Teachers of English. *Raising Readers: A Guide to Sharing Literature with Young Children*. Walker, 1980.

Written by a committee, this guide tells parents how they can help their young children acquire the reading habit and make reading a lifelong joy. Annotated lists of carefully chosen books accompany details of the various stages of child development.

Oppenheim, Joanne, Barbara Brenner, and Betty D. Boegehold. *Choosing Books for Kids: Choosing the Right Book for the Right Child at the Right Time*. Ballantine Books, 1986.

The subtitle of this Bank Street College of Education publication sums up its purpose—to match books to children's stages of development.

Segal, Marilyn, and Don Adcock. *Your Child at Play: One to Two Years*. Newmarket Press, 1985.

Language-enhancement activities, including reading aloud and conversational play, are incorporated in this basic child-rearing guide.

Trelease, Jim. *The New Read-Aloud Handbook*, 2nd ed. Penguin Books, 1989.

Trelease shows that reading aloud can make a lasting difference to children by teaching them to want to read. Included is an annotated list of over 300 titles, from picture books for infants to adult books suitable for teenagers.

3. Books Alive! Sharing Books with Young Children

NELL COLBURN

INTENDED AUDIENCE: Family caregivers—people who provide child care in a home environment

LENGTH: Three hours, with a twenty minute break

SUMMARY OF PROGRAM: This talk was designed to convince family caregivers of the importance of making books a part of young children's daily lives and to present the public library as a valuable and user-friendly community resource. Throughout the talk my emphasis is on the exciting variety of books available for young children today. I identify books appropriate for specific ages and introduce well-known authors and illustrators who have produced many books for young children. I also try to demonstrate how to read and share books, songs, and rhymes with young children.

The talk originated as the first session in a four-part series titled *Books Alive! A Series of Talks and Workshops for Family Caregivers*. The three subsequent sessions were hands-on workshops about bringing books alive through the use of flannel board storytelling, simple puppets and crafts, and creative dramatics and music.

I sometimes present the first part of this talk as "Sharing Books with Infants and Toddlers," a one-session program advertised for new and expectant parents.

HINTS FOR PLANNING AND PRESENTATION
Promotion
The success of this program depends on strong publicity. You may want to attend Family Caregiver Association meetings or local licensing meetings for caregivers. Introduce yourself and show some enticing materials—books on toilet training, sibling rivalry, or the death of a pet—or perhaps share a flannel board story. Take the opportunity to invite people to the program personally. It is likely that many of them have never set foot inside a library. Once they see that there is a good reason to do so—and that there will be a pleasant, smiling librarian to help them—they will be much more willing to sign up for a program than if they had just seen an advertis-

ing flyer or poster. You also will want to get an announcement in newsletters read by the family caregiver community.

Planning

As preparation for this kind of program you may want to read Dorothy Butler's *Babies Need Books*[1] and Nancy Larrick's *A Parent's Guide to Children's Reading.*[2] Larrick, and later Butler, convinced me that children's librarians should be programming for parents and adults who work with children. This talk grew out of their ideas.

Presentation

Because the intended audience may have working hours ranging from 6 a.m. to 6 p.m., Monday through Friday, the program should be presented in the evening or on a Saturday.

The best part of the program is the actual sharing of the books. Read several books aloud, all the way through, and show parts of others. Don't be shy about this. Everyone always loves it and the books you present are the ones that people will remember and seek out.

Try to involve the group as much possible. Invite everyone to join you in learning a tickling rhyme or simple action song such as "Where Is Thumbkin?"

In the sections of my talk about authors and illustrators, I introduce each author and illustrator using the book indicated. I point out distinctive aspects of style as I go through the book. I emphasize that each of these people has produced many fine works for children and that their books would be a good place to start when approaching the library's huge picture book collection. I also like to point out that their books can be found in most public libraries in the country.

Leave time at the end of the program to give a tour of the library or the children's area. Using the bibliography, demonstrate how easy it is to find the picture books you have discussed. Have library card applications available.

I. INTRODUCTION

    A. Discuss the importance of introducing children to books at an early age.

        1. Researchers have discovered that by age four, fifty percent of a person's intelligence has developed; and another thirty percent, by age eight.[3] The foundation for all future learning is laid during the early years of life. You and I work with young

---

1. Dorothy Butler, *Babies Need Books* (New York: Atheneum, 1980).

2. Nancy Larrick, *A Parent's Guide to Children's Reading*, 5th ed. (New York: Bantam, 1982).

3. Dorothy Butler, *Babies Need Books*, 1.

children every day. We inevitably play a key role in laying that foundation.

2. My experience as a children's librarian has convinced me that books must be a part of every child's early years. I have seen that children who are exposed to books in the preschool years grow up to be good listeners, good speakers, good readers, and intelligent, sensitive human beings.

3. During a child's early years, we can instill the desire for books. This desire must be there before a child can learn to read. The child must *want* to read.

B. Underline the need for an adult to bring children and books together.

1. Children cannot discover the delights of books on their own; they need an adult to bring books into their lives and help them see that books and reading are fun—just like riding a bicycle or playing baseball is fun. It's up to those of us who spend our days with young children to introduce them to books, to make books a natural part of their everyday world, to give them memorable experiences with books.

2. What is the best time to start using books with young children? In the first weeks, and first months of their lives.

II. IN THE BEGINNING: 1 WEEK TO 1½ YEARS

A. Recommend song books as first books for a baby. Songs provide an early, delightful language experience: baby hears lots of words, and begins to develop a feeling for the patterns of our language.

1. Show the variety of lullabies and morning songs in *The Fireside Book of Children's Songs* and in *Singing Bee! A Collection of Favorite Children's Songs*.

2. Demonstrate songs for crib play. Show *Eye Winker, Tom Tinker,* and demonstrate fingerplay for "Where Is Thumbkin?" and "Pop Goes the Weasel." Baby hears how a question is phrased: "Where is Thumbkin?" Baby hears how an answer is phrased: "Here I am!"

3. Show how songs can provide a first encounter with basic concepts. For example, use "This Old Man" to introduce numbers and "Put Your Finger in the Air" to introduce body parts.

B. Show a selection of Mother Goose books and nursery rhyme collections. These rhymes offer more wonderful words for baby as well as marvelous sounds and rhythms.

1. Lots of these rhymes relate to baby's daily activities. For exam-

ple, say "One, Two, Buckle My Shoe" while dressing baby; or "Rub-a-Dub-Dub" at bath time.

2. Many rhymes reinforce words the child hears daily, such as tub, rain, up, down, shoe, and bake. Others introduce less familiar words. My favorite words from Mother Goose are: contrary, blithe, horrid, crooked, delve, tattered, dainty, and nimble. At first these words just sound good to baby; their meaning comes through eventually, without effort.

3. It's fun to compare the art in several different Mother Goose books. Older children will enjoy deciding which picture of Humpty or Little Miss Muffet they like best. Be sure to talk with them about why they like it.

4. Show Montgomerie's *This Little Pig Went to Market*, a book of tickling rhymes, knee bouncers, foot pats, and leg waggers. Demonstrate a tickling rhyme. Montgomerie explains that the actions used to accompany the rhymes illustrate the abstract words for baby. The strength of this book is that it shows us how to have fun with nursery rhymes. Once you get the idea, you will be looking for knee bouncing and tickling rhymes throughout the nursery rhyme collection.

C. Show a sampling of first picture books. Use these as soon as baby is able to focus. A child will enjoy looking at the bright colors, and simple shapes.

1. Look for books in which text is minimal; and the emphasis is on the illustrations.
   Show:
   Rabbit's Morning
   Across the Stream
   Brown Bear, Brown Bear, What Do You See?

2. Many picture books combine lovely illustrations with a poetic text. Read or sing these while you show the pictures.
   Show:
   Goodnight, Moon
   Hush Little Baby

D. Introduce board books. Use these when a child reaches the grabbing and tearing stage. They can be wiped clean and are almost chew resistant.

1. Thick, easily turned pages let little ones explore just how a book works—how it starts in the beginning, and how it reads from left to right. The best of the board books have some appeal for adults as well as little ones.

Show:
   Friends
   Playing

   2. Explain how these books are meant to be talked about, not read. Use the pictures as a springboard for talk about colors, numbers, shapes, or a child's experiences and environment. Show:
   Things I Like to Wear

E. Discuss I Spy Books. Show Ogle's *I Spy* and demonstrate various ways to play the I Spy game (see Ogle's introduction). Suggest using the same methods with catalogs and magazines. The idea is to name things, to give the child words. Many authors and illustrators have produced books that librarians call I Spy or naming books. Each of the following people has delighted children with more than one.
   Authors and illustrators to know
      Allan Ahlberg and Janet Ahlberg (Show *Peek-a-Boo!*)
      Gyo Fujikawa (Show *A to Z Picture Book*)
      Peter Spier (Show *Gobble Growl Grunt*)

III. TODDLERS: 1+ TO 3 YEARS

A. Show a selection of short picture books. Look for stories with lots of action and minimal description. Each of the following authors and illustrators has produced several very special books for young children.
   Authors and illustrators to know
      Margaret Wise Brown (Read part of *The Runaway Bunny*)
      John Burningham (Read *Mr. Gumpy's Outing*)
      Pat Hutchins (Read *Titch*)
      Eve Rice (Read *Benny Bakes a Cake*)

B. Discuss simple concept books. These emphasize colors, numbers, shapes, size, days of the week, etc.
   Authors and illustrators to know
      Molly Bang (Read *Ten, Nine, Eight*)
      Eric Carle (Read *The Very Hungry Caterpillar*)
      Donald Crews (Read *Freight Train*)
      Tana Hoban (Show *Of Colors and Things*)

C. Introduce participation books. These are designed to pull young listeners right into the story. They are irresistible.
   Authors and illustrators to know
      Eric Hill (Read *Where's Spot?*)
      Shigeo Watanabe (Read *How Do I Put It On?*)

IV. GROWING, GROWING: 3 TO 5 YEARS

A. Show a selection of longer picture books. These offer more complicated stories and longer texts for growing attention spans.
Authors and illustrators to know
Paul Galdone (Show *The Three Bears*)
Russell Hoban (Show *Bedtime for Frances*)
Shirley Hughes (Read part of *Alfie Gives a Hand*)
Ezra Jack Keats (Read part of *Whistle for Willie*; show *The Snowy Day*)
Robert McCloskey (Show *Make Way for Ducklings*)
Maurice Sendak (Read *Where the Wild Things Are*)

B. Discuss simple information books. These offer words and pictures to help the child pin down an expanding world of ideas and experiences.
Authors and illustrators to know
Byron Barton (Show *Airport* and *Building A House*)
Gail Gibbons (Show *Trucks*)
Tana Hoban (Show *A Children's Zoo*)
Anne Rockwell (Show *Fire Engines*)

C. Show a selection of wordless picture books. These encourage language development and logical thinking by requiring children to tell the story in their own words.
Authors and illustrators to know
John Goodall (Show *The Adventures of Paddy Pork*)
Mercer Mayer (Show *A Boy, a Dog and a Frog*)
Jan Ormerod (Show *Sunshine and Moonlight*)

D. Discuss picture books on special subjects. In recent years publishers have produced more picture books on special subjects, such as new baby in the family, death, hospitalization, death of a pet, divorce, and adoption. I am glad to see this because:

1. I think that understanding something is the key to being able to cope with it. These books can help a child understand a particular problem or emotion.

2. These books can provide reassurance to a child concerned about being the only one jealous of a new baby or anxious about the first day of school.

3. These books also show children that their feelings or situations are important enough to have whole books written about them.

4. Often, books like these can help an adult talk to a child about a particular problem.

Authors and illustrators to know
  Marc Brown (Show *Dinosaurs Divorce*)
  Lucille Clifton (Read part of *Everett Anderson's Nine
    Months Long*)
  Joanna Cole (Show *The New Baby at Your House*)
  Harlow Rockwell (Show *My Dentist* and *My Doctor*)
  Fred Rogers (Show *Going to the Potty* and *Going to Day
    Care*)
  Judith Viorst (Read *The Tenth Good Thing about Barney*)

V. TIME FOR QUESTIONS AND DISCUSSION; OFFER TOUR OF
LIBRARY WITH EMPHASIS ON HOW TO LOCATE THE PIC-
TURE BOOKS DISCUSSED

A Sampler of Books to Share with Young Children

In the Beginning: 1 Week to 1½ Years

Song Books

Glazer, Tom. *Eye Winker, Tom Tinker, Chin Chopper: Fifty Musical Fin-
  gerplays*. Doubleday, 1973.
Hart, Jane, ed. *Singing Bee! A Collection of Favorite Children's Songs*.
  Lothrop, 1982.
Winn, Marie, ed. *The Fireside Book of Children's Songs*. Simon and
  Schuster, 1966.

Mother Goose and Nursery Rhymes

Briggs, Raymond, illus. *The Mother Goose Treasury*. Putnam, 1966.
De Angeli, Marguerite. *Marguerite De Angeli's Book of Nursery and Moth-
  er Goose Rhymes*. Doubleday, 1954.
dePaola, Tomie, illus. *Tomie dePaola's Mother Goose*. Putnam, 1985.
Hague, Michael, illus. *Mother Goose: A Collection of Classic Nursery
  Rhymes*. Holt, 1984.
Lobel, Arnold, illus. *The Random House Book of Mother Goose: A Treas-
  ury of 306 Timeless Nursery Rhymes*. Random, 1986.
Provensen, Alice, and Martin Provensen, illus. *The Mother Goose Book*.
  Random, 1976.
Rojankovsky, Feodor, illus. *The Tall Book of Mother Goose*. Harper, 1942.
*This Little Pig Went to Market: Play Rhymes for Infants and Young Chil-
  dren*. Comp. by Norah Montgomerie. The Bodley Head, 1966.
Wildsmith, Brian, illus. *Brian Wildsmith's Mother Goose*. Oxford, 1982.
Wright, Blanche Fisher, illus. *The Real Mother Goose*. Macmillan, 1987.

First Picture Books

Aliki, illus. *Hush Little Baby: A Folk Lullaby*. Prentice-Hall, 1968.
Brown, Margaret Wise. *Goodnight, Moon*. Harper, 1947.
Ginsburg, Mirra. *Across The Stream*. Greenwillow, 1982.
Martin, Bill. *Brown Bear, Brown Bear, What Do You See?* Illus. by Eric Carle. Holt 1983.
Tafuri, Nancy. *Rabbit's Morning*. Greenwillow, 1985.

Board Books

Oxenbury, Helen. *Friends*. Wanderer, 1981.
———. *Playing*. Wanderer, 1981.
Zokeisha. *Things I Like to Wear*. Simon and Schuster, 1981.

I Spy Books

Ahlberg, Allan, and Janet Ahlberg. *Peek-a-Boo!* Viking, 1981.
Fujikawa, Gyo. *A to Z Picture Book*. Putnam, 1974.
Ogle, Lucille, and Tina Throburn. *I Spy with My Little Eye: A Picture Book of Objects in a Child's Home Environment*. Illus. by Joe Kaufman. McGraw, 1970.
Spier, Peter. *Gobble Growl Grunt*. Doubleday, 1988.

Toddlers: 1½ to 3 Years

Short Picture Books

Brown, Margaret Wise. *The Runaway Bunny*. Harper, 1972.
Burningham, John. *Mr. Gumpy's Outing*. Holt, 1971.
Hutchins, Pat. *Titch*. Macmillan, 1971.
Rice, Eve. *Benny Bakes a Cake*. Greenwillow, 1981.

Simple Concept Books

Bang, Molly. *Ten, Nine, Eight*. Greenwillow, 1983.
Carle, Eric. *The Very Hungry Caterpillar*. Putnam, 1981.
Crews, Donald. *Freight Train*. Greenwillow, 1978.
Hoban, Tana. *Of Colors and Things*. Greenwillow, 1989.

Participation Books

Hill, Eric. *Where's Spot?* Putnam, 1980.
Watanabe, Shigeo. *How Do I Put It On?* Illus. by Yasuo Ohtomo. Putnam, 1984.

Growing, Growing: 3 to 5 Years

Longer Picture Books

Galdone, Paul. *The Three Bears*. Houghton Mifflin, 1972.
Hoban, Russell. *Bedtime for Frances*. Harper, 1960.
Hughes, Shirley. *Alfie Gives a Hand*. Lothrop, 1984.
Keats, Ezra Jack. *The Snowy Day*. Viking, 1962.
————. *Whistle for Willie*. Viking, 1964.
McCloskey, Robert. *Make Way for Ducklings*. Viking, 1941.
Sendak, Maurice. *Where the Wild Things Are*. Harper, 1963.

Simple Information Books

Barton, Byron. *Airport*. Crowell, 1982.
————. *Building a House*. Greenwillow, 1981.
Gibbons, Gail. *Trucks*. Crowell, 1981.
Hoban, Tana. *A Children's Zoo*. Greenwillow, 1985.
Rockwell, Anne. *Fire Engines*. Dutton, 1986.

Wordless Picture Books

Goodall, John. *The Adventures of Paddy Pork*. Harcourt, 1968.
Mayer, Mercer. *A Boy, a Dog and a Frog*. Dial, 1971.
Ormerod, Jan. *Moonlight*. Lothrop, 1982.
————. *Sunshine*. Lothrop, 1981.

Picture Books on Special Subjects

Brown, Laurene K., and Marc Brown. *Dinosaurs Divorce: A Guide for
Changing Families*. Little, 1986.
Clifton, Lucille. *Everett Anderson's Nine Months Long*. Illus. by Ann Gri-
falconi. Holt, 1978.
Cole, Joanna. *The New Baby at Your House*. Photos by Hella Hammid.
Morrow, 1985.
Rockwell, Harlow. *My Dentist*. Greenwillow, 1975.
————. *My Doctor*. Macmillan, 1973.
Rogers, Fred. *Going to Day Care*. Photographs by Jim Judkis. Putnam,
1985.
————. *Going to the Potty*. Photographs by Jim Judkis. Putnam, 1985.
Viorst, Judith. *The Tenth Good Thing about Barney*. Illus. by Erik Blegvad.
Atheneum, 1971.

4. Start with a Story: Circle Time for Preschoolers

HARRIET HERSCHEL

INTENDED AUDIENCE: High school students

LENGTH: One hour and ten minutes

SUMMARY OF PROGRAM: This talk was designed to be given to high school students studying child development in a home economics class. The class was preparing to do field work in a day care center, where they would be sharing picture books with preschoolers during circle time.

Objectives of this program were to generate enthusiasm and appreciation for picture books among the students, to teach them how to share the books with young children during circle time, and to help them understand the services and assistance available to them from the public library.

HINTS FOR PLANNING AND PRESENTATION: For best results, seat the students in a semi-circle around you. Make sure that you read at least three picture books. High school students will particularly enjoy a participation story, such as *Where's Spot?* or *Would You Rather?* Do not show the suggested movie if your time with a group is limited or your program site does not lend itself to the viewing of a film; concentrate on your own presentation.

Editors' Note: Sue McCleaf-Nespeca often presents a three-hour version of Herschel's seventy-minute program. Like Herschel, McCleaf-Nespeca begins her program with an hour devoted to the basics of reading aloud to groups of preschoolers. After a thirty-minute break, she discusses special techniques, such as flannel board storytelling and tell-and-draw storytelling. She then booktalks a varied selection of titles that she feels would be of special interest to early childhood educators and caregivers. She includes source books such as Judy Nichols' *Storytimes for Two-Year-Olds*, as well as fingerplay, puppet, song, and easy craft books. The extensive annotated bibliographies from which she draws her booktalks are appended to this section.

I. INTRODUCTION

    A. Discuss your work with young children, emphasizing your experience with circle time.

    B. As a warm-up, talk to the students about their experiences with picture books. Ask them about books they remember from their preschool years.

II. FILM VIEWING
Show the film *What's So Great about Books*, which conveys the importance of reading to children and gives valuable suggestions for reading-related activities.[1]

III. SHARING PICTURE BOOKS

    A. Briefly discuss types of picture books, referring to the bibliography which follows this outline.

    B. Present the benefits of reading picture books to young children.
        1. To help young children with the process of learning to read.
        2. To introduce youngsters to many new words, promoting language development.
        3. To provide a pleasurable experience for both you and the children.

    C. Read three books from the bibliography you have distributed to the group.

    D. Discuss some of the techniques of reading picture books.
        1. Demonstrate the proper way to hold the books.
        2. Demonstrate how to read with meaning and enthusiasm, emphasizing that you have to like a book if you are going to share it with a group successfully.
        3. Demonstrate how to use your voice for clarity, enjoyment, and suspense.

IV. FINGERPLAYS

    A. Explain why fingerplays are necessary for circle time.
        1. Parents, teachers, day care providers and librarians have found that fingerplays are successful and entertaining activities.

---

1. *What's So Great about Books*, 16 mm (Orlando Public Library, 1977). Distributed by Cypress Films.

2. They help with a young child's development.
   a. They help a child learn the language.
   b. They improve motor dexterity and coordination.
3. They can be used to extend a story.
4. They relieve restlessness and allow children to let out energy.
5. They can be used as a transition between a story and a song, creative dramatic activity, a filmstrip, or another story.

B. Demonstrate "Here Is the Beehive" from *Wee Sing: Children's Songs and Fingerplays* by Pamela Conn Beall and Susan Hagen Nipp.[2]

C. Refer to the fingerplay bibliography for a brief discussion of fingerplay and action-rhyme sources. You may want to provide the bibliography as a handout.

V. PUPPETRY

A. Explain why you would use puppets in circle time.
1. Children are naturally drawn to puppets.
2. There is a magical quality about puppets that makes learning enjoyable for children.
3. Puppetry for young children is valuable as a means of communication and self-expression. Even the shyest child will open up to a puppet.

B. Talk about the variety of types of puppets.
1. Finger puppets.
2. Stick puppets.
3. Hand puppets.
4. Puppets made by children.

C. Demonstrate storytelling with puppets. I like to tell *The Gunniwolf.*

D. Refer to the puppet and puppetry bibliography for a brief discussion of some of the books on the subject. You may also duplicate the bibliography and distribute it as a handout.

VI. CREATIVE DRAMATICS

A. Define creative dramatics and explain why it is an important activity.
1. The use of creative dramatics makes a good break during a circle time.

2. Pamela Conn Beall and Susan Hagen Nipp, *Wee Sing: Children's Songs and Fingerplays* (Los Angeles, Calif.: Price, Stern, Sloan, 1979).

2. Creative dramatic activities allow children to use their imaginations.

B. Give hints on how to make creative dramatics successful.

1. Keep the activity simple.

2. Although it is not necessary, the activity can be related to the stories.

3. Remember that this is an activity for fun and exercise; it is not supposed to be formal drama.

C. Demonstrate, using students from the class, how the story of *Peace at Last* can be acted out.[3]

VII. FILMS

A. Explain why you use films in circle time.

1. It is good to expose children to a variety of media.

2. Films help children develop a critical eye.

B. Show a short film such as *Rosie's Walk*, which runs five minutes.[4]

Circle Time Favorites

Mother Goose and Nursery Rhymes

dePaola, Tomie. *Tomie dePaola's Mother Goose*. Putnam, 1985.
Lobel, Arnold. *Gregory Griggs and Other Nursery Rhyme People*.
   Greenwillow, 1978.
Wright, Blanche. *Real Mother Goose*. Macmillan, 1916.

ABC and Counting Books

Anno, Mitsumasa. *Anno's Counting Book*. Harper, 1977.
Bang, Molly. *Ten, Nine, Eight*. Greenwillow, 1983.
Lobel, Arnold. *On Market Street*. Greenwillow, 1981.
Wildsmith, Brian. *ABC*. Watts, 1962.

Concept Books

Carle, Eric. *The Very Hungry Caterpillar*. Putnam, 1981.
Crews, Donald. *Freight Train*. Greenwillow, 1978.
Hoban, Tana. *I Read Signs*. Greenwillow, 1983.
Kalan, Robert. *Rain*. Illus. by Donald Crews. Greenwillow, 1978.
Shaw, Charles. *It Looked like Spilt Milk*. Harper, 1988.

3. Jill Murphy, *Peace at Last* (New York: Dial, 1970).
4. *Rosie's Walk* (Westport, Conn.: Weston Woods).

Plots That Relate to a Child's Experience

Breinburg, Petronella. *Shawn Goes to School*. Crowell, 1974.
Hughes, Shirley. *Alfie Gets In First*. Lothrop, 1982.
Hutchins, Pat. *Happy Birthday, Sam*. Greenwillow, 1978.
Keats, Ezra Jack. *Peter's Chair*. Harper, 1967.
McCloskey, Robert. *Blueberries for Sal*. Viking, 1948.
Rice, Eve. *What Sadie Sang*. Greenwillow, 1976.
Yashima, Taro. *Umbrella*. Viking, 1958.

Fanciful Plots Still Related to a Child's Experience

Freeman, Don. *Corduroy*. Viking, 1968.
Rylant, Cynthia. *The Relatives Came*. Illus. by Stephen Gammill.
    Bradbury, 1985.
Sendak, Maurice. *Where the Wild Things Are*. Harper, 1963.
Slobodkina, Esphyr. *Caps for Sale*. Scott, 1968.
Wood, Audrey. *King Bidgood's in the Bathtub*. Illus. by Don Wood.
    Harcourt, 1985.

Just for Fun

Barrett, Judith. *Animals Should Definitely Not Wear Clothes*. Illus. by Ron
    Barrett. Atheneum, 1970.
Burningham, John. *Would You Rather?* Harper, 1978.
Hill, Eric. *Where's Spot?* Putnam, 1980.
Murphy, Jill. *Peace at Last*. Dial, 1980.

Cumulative Stories

Gag, Wanda. *Millions of Cats*. Putnam, 1977.
Harper, Wilhelmena. *Gunniwolf*. Illus. by William Wiesner. Dutton, 1967.
Scheer, Julian. *Rain Makes Applesauce*. Illus. by Marvin Bileck. Holiday,
    1964.

Folk Tales

Bang, Molly. *Wiley and the Hairy Man*. Macmillan, 1976.
Galdone, Paul. *The Three Billy Goats Gruff*. Houghton Mifflin, 1981.
Marshall, James. *Red Riding Hood*. Dial, 1987.

Picture Books of Single Songs

Aliki, illus. *Hush Little Baby: A Folk Lullaby*. Prentice-Hall, 1968.
Langstaff, John. *Oh A-Hunting We Will Go*. Atheneum, 1983.
Westcott, Nadine B. *The Lady with the Alligator Purse*. Little, 1988.
———. *There Was an Old Lady Who Swallowed a Fly*. Little, 1980.

Fun for Older Kids

Allard, Harry. *Miss Nelson Is Missing*. Illus. by James Marshall. Houghton Mifflin, 1977.

Steig, William. *Doctor DeSoto*. Farrar, 1982.

Van Allsburg, Chris. *Jumanji*. Houghton Mifflin, 1981.

Williams, Vera. *A Chair for My Mother*. Greenwillow, 1982.

Preparation for Circle Time

Fingerplays

Beall, Pamela, and Susan Nipp. *Wee Sing: Children's Songs and Fingerplays*. Price, Stern, Sloan, 1982.
A popular collection of familiar songs and fingerplays. A cassette is included.

Brown, Marc. *Finger Rhymes*. Dutton, 1980.
Fourteen traditional rhymes with directions for finger actions in picture book format. *Hand Rhymes*, by the same author, is similar (Dutton, 1985).

Glazer, Tom. *Eye Winker, Tom Tinker, Chin Chopper: Fifty Musical Fingerplays*. Doubleday, 1973.
Simple action songs and fingerplays set to music.

Grayson, Marion. *Let's Do Fingerplays*. Luce, 1962.
A comprehensive collection of nearly two hundred fingerplays arranged by subject.

Montgomerie, Norah. *This Little Pig Went to Market: Play Rhymes for Infants and Young Children*. The Bodley Head, 1966.
Action rhymes, fingerplays, singing games, and lap games for the youngest.

Ring a Ring o' Roses: Finger Plays for Preschool Children. 9th ed. Flint Public Library (91026 E. Kearsley, Flint, MI 48502).
A favorite of librarians, this extensive collection of fingerplays is arranged by subject and includes a first-line index.

Scott, Louise Binder, and J. J. Thompson. *Rhymes for Fingers and Flannelboards*. McGraw-Hill, 1960.
Organized by subject, this offers explicit directions for flannel board variations, including a few fingerplays in Spanish and French, and one each in Italian, Japanese, and German.

Tashjian, Virginia. *Juba This and Juba That: Story Hour Stretches for Large and Small Groups*. Little, 1969.
Rhymes, fingerplays, chants, short games, and participation stories.

Puppets, Poetry, and Creative Dramatics

Champlin, Connie. *Puppetry and Creative Dramatics in Storytelling*. Renfro Studios, 1980.

Simple puppetry and creative dramatics combine to bring stories to life.

————, and Nancy Renfro. *Storytelling with Puppets*. American Library Association, 1985.

Basic puppetry construction and skills with a variety of suggestions for storytelling.

Chernoff, Goldie Taub. *Puppet Party*. Walker, 1971.

A charming, how-to-do-puppetry book, presented in picture-book format. This features easy, inexpensive puppets of cloth and paper.

Engler, Larry, and Carol Fijan. *Making Puppets Come Alive: A Method of Learning and Teaching Hand Puppetry*. Taplinger, 1973.

Illustrated with helpful photographs, this was specifically conceived to teach beginners how to bring a hand puppet to life and how to mount an amateur puppet show.

Gates, Frieda. *Glove, Mitten and Sock Puppets*. Walker, 1978.

With clear, brief directions, these clever ideas for quick puppets utilize easily available materials, such as yarn, buttons, and old socks.

Hunt, Tamara, and Nancy Renfro. *Puppetry in Early Childhood Education*. Renfro Studios, 1982.

Lots of ideas and patterns for puppetry with the young child. Includes a useful list of stories that make good puppet shows and a comprehensive bibliography of puppet organizations, manufacturers, suppliers, and puppetry books and pamphlets.

Jagendorf, Moritz. *Puppets for Beginners*. Plays, 1952.

This slim book illustrates how to make a variety of puppets from common household materials.

Lewis, Shari. *Making Easy Puppets*. Dutton, 1967.

An accomplished puppeteer shares her world of simple-to-construct puppets. Helpful photographs and drawings demonstrate how the puppets are made.

McCaslin, Nellie. *Puppet Fun*. McKay, 1977.

Instructions for making easy puppets and producing a variety of plays, including good suggestions for making up one's own plays.

McLaren, Esme. *Making Glove Puppets*. Plays, 1973.

All kinds of glove puppets, perfect for small shows in school or at home. The costumes illustrated are easy to construct, making McLaren's book a hit with mothers and caregivers.

Paludan, Lis. *Playing with Puppets*. Plays, 1975.

Instructions for paper bag, spoon, vegetable, sock, and glove puppets, as well as instructions for theater construction and play writing.

Wilt, Joy, and Gwen Hurn. *Puppets with Pizazz: 52 Finger and Hand Puppets Children Can Make and Use.* Creative Resources, 1977.
Good patterns for easily and inexpensively made puppets.

Early Childhood Resources

Contributed by Sue McCleaf-Nespeca

Beall, Pamela, and Susan Nipp. *Wee Sing: Children's Songs and Fingerplays.* Price, Stern, Sloan, 1982.
A collection of fingerplays, and children's songs with music and guitar chords particularly useful for those looking for old favorites. A cassette is included.

Broad, Laura P., and Nancy T. Butterworth. *The Playgroup Handbook.* St. Martin's, 1974.
Though the first part of the book deals specifically with organizing a neighborhood playgroup, the second longer part will be useful to anyone working with young children. Includes arts and crafts, dramatic plays, music, physical education, games, and science activities for each month of the year.

Brown, Marc. *Finger Rhymes.* Dutton, 1980.
Fourteen familiar fingerplays on how to perform each rhyme.

Cole, Ann. *I Saw a Purple Cow.* Little, 1972.
100 "recipes for learning" cover the subjects of creating, pretending, exploring, music and rhythm, parties, and learning games. Many ideas are centered around a child's everyday experiences and require only a few household items.

————, and Carolyn Haas. *Purple Cow to the Rescue.* Little, 1982.
Similar to its predecessor listed above, this newer title contains recipes dealing with getting to know and like yourself, learning to be independent, learning basics, traveling, and moving.

Dowell, Ruth I. *Move Over, Mother Goose: Finger Plays, Action Verses and Funny Rhymes.* Gryphon, 1987.
Fingerplays, action verses, and funny rhymes with motions included.

Forte, Imogene. *Kids' Stuff Book of Patterns, Projects, and Plans to Perk Up Early Learning Programs.* Incentive Publications, 1982.
A book of reproducible patterns for teachers on subjects such as seasons and holidays, animal antics, and "things that go." Teaching suggestions and pupil-activity pages are included.

Glazer, Tom. *Do Your Ears Hang Low?* Doubleday, 1980.
Words and music to fifty songs that can be performed as fingerplays. Includes music for the piano and chords for the guitar, banjo, and autoharp.

————. *Eye Winker, Tom Tinker, Chin Chopper: Fifty Musical Fingerplays.* Doubleday, 1973.

Identical in format to the sequel described above, this is Glazer's popular, original work.

————. *Music for Ones and Twos: Songs and Games for the Very Young.* Doubleday, 1983.

Fifty six songs, games and fingerplays for the very young child. Includes music and guitar chords.

Graham, Terry. *Let Loose on Mother Goose.* Incentive Publications, 1982.

Mother Goose nursery rhymes are used to teach music, art, creative dramatics, language development, math, science, and related activities.

Haas, Carolyn. *Recipes for Fun and Learning: Creative Learning Activities for Young Children.* CBH Publishing, 1982.

These creative open-ended learning activities include arts and crafts projects, science and nature projects, and much more.

Hart, Jane, ed. *Singing Bee! A Collection of Favorite Children's Songs.* Lothrop, 1982.

A well-rounded collection of over 100 favorite children's songs, lullabies, Mother Goose rhymes, and folk songs, with piano arrangements and guitar chords. Illustrations by award-winning artist Anita Lobel.

Hunt, Tamara, and Nancy Renfro. *Celebrate! Holidays, Puppets and Creative Drama.* Renfro Studios, 1987.

Ideas for holiday activities presented in a month-by-month approach. Includes eleven international holidays.

————. *Puppetry in Early Childhood Education.* Renfro Studios, 1981.

A complete guide to puppetry for early childhood teachers with many illustrations, suggestions for puppet making and teaching, puppetry, and sources for materials.

Indenbaum, Valerie, and Marcia Shapiro. *The Everything Book: For Teachers of Young Children.* Revised ed. Partner Press, 1985.

A month-by-month approach including arts and crafts, stories, cooking projects, fingerplays, activities for physical development, games, and field trip suggestions. A comprehensive guide for early-childhood teachers.

Kohl, Mary Ann F. *Scribble Cookies and Other Independent Creative Art Experiences for Children.* Bright Ring, 1985.

Using materials such as paper, chalk, crayons, paint, clay, wood, string, and foil, these 119 open-ended projects will encourage children to experiment with various artistic mediums.

Matterson, Elizabeth, comp. *Games for the Very Young: Finger Plays and Nursery Games.* American Heritage, 1969.

Games, fingerplays and nursery songs, some accompanied by music, for more than two hundred rhymes babies and preschoolers enjoy.

Marzollo, Jean, and Janice Lloyd. *Learning through Play.* Harper, 1972.

Though designed for parents to use at home, many of these learning activities, games, and play ideas could be incorporated into an early-childhood program.

Nelson, Esther. *Funny Songbook*. Sterling, 1984.

———. *Silly Songbook*. Sterling, 1981.

Each collection contains over fifty humorous songs with piano arrangements and guitar chords. Many are old favorites sung at camps, Bible schools, and other group gatherings.

Newmann, Dana. *Early Childhood Teacher's Almanac: Activities for Every Month of the Year*. Center for Applied Research in Education, 1984.

A month-by-month planning guide for early-childhood teachers, including suggestions for crafts, stories, recipes, and field trips.

Peterson, Betty J. *Collection of Everyday Art Projects*. Betty J. Peterson, 1973.

Arranged by season, more than fifty art projects for early-childhood teachers. Includes a special section of recipes for paint, modeling dough, clay, papier mâché, and other materials.

Price, Lowi, and Marilyn Wronsky. *Recipes for Creeping Crystals, Invisible Ink, Self-Stick Plastic, Grease Paint, Playdough and Other Inedibles*. Dutton, 1976.

Recipes for making a variety of interesting concoctions from household ingredients.

Raffi. *Raffi Singable Songbook*. Crown, 1987.

From the albums of the popular Canadian folksinger, fifty-one songs with guitar and piano arrangements.

Renfro, Nancy. *Bags Are Big: A Paper Bag Craft Book*. Renfro Studios, 1983.

Objects to make with common brown grocery bags.

Ring a Ring o' Roses: Finger Plays for Preschool Children. 9th ed. Flint Public Library (91026 E. Kearsley, Flint, MI 40852).

Hundreds of fingerplays and action rhymes, divided by themes and accompanied by directions on how to perform each rhyme.

Roberts, Lynda. *Mitt Magic: Fingerplays for Finger Puppets*. Gryphon House, 1986.

More than fifty-five fingerplays, including several for holidays, with patterns for making finger puppets and a glove puppet.

Rockwell, Anne. *Games and How to Play Them*. Harper, 1973.

Including the familiar and the less familiar, forty-three active games for the very young child, complemented by bright, colorful animal illustrations.

Rudolph, Marguerita. *From Hand to Head*. Schocken Books, 1973.

This handbook for teachers of preschool programs includes cooking, nature, transportation, safety, art, and other activities for the young child.

Sattler, Helen R. *Recipes for Art and Craft Materials*. Revised ed. Lothrop, 1987.
Similar to *Concoctions*, listed above, but including more complicated recipes for pastes, modeling compounds, papier mâché, paints, inks, casting compounds, and dried flower preservatives. This book is for parents, teachers, or youth group leaders.

Scott, Louise Binder. *Rhymes for Learning Times*. Denison, 1983.
Rhymes for the whole body or just for fingers, along with directions on how to perform the activities.

————, and J. J. Thompson. *Rhymes for Fingers and Flannelboards*. McGraw-Hill, 1960.
Directions for fingerplays and instructions on how to convert the rhymes into flannel board activities.

Stangl, Jean. *Paper Stories*. David S. Lake, 1981.
The Chinese art of making paper cutouts while telling a story is featured in this book of thirty-one original stories and poems. Included are reproducible patterns for the cutouts.

Stauros, Sally, and Ruth Bell. *Big Learning for Little Learners: Easy Guide for Teaching Early Childhood Activities*. Partner Press, 1987.
A month-by-month guide for early-childhood educators similar to *The Everything Book* described above. Included are art, literature, music, science, social studies, physical education, math, and cooking activities along with suggestions of books to read aloud.

Wilmes, Liz, and Dick Wilmes. *Felt Board Fun*. Building Blocks, 1984.
Instructions for making a felt board and felt board pieces along with units for early childhood teachers that deal with concepts such as food, the body, animals, seasons, and individual holidays.

Winn, Marie. *What Shall We Do and Allee Galloo! Play Songs and Singing Games for Young Children*. Harper, 1970.
Follow-the-leader songs, word-play songs, fingerplay and motion songs, and simple game songs for preschool children. Included are piano arrangements, guitar chords, and directions on how to perform the activities.

Storytelling Books

Contributed by Sue McCleaf-Nespeca

Anderson, Paul S. *Storytelling with the Flannel Board*. Book 1, Denison, 1963.
————. *Storytelling with the Flannel Board*. Book 2, Denison, 1970.
Original stories and old favorites accompanied by drawings that can be made into flannel board pieces.

Baker, Augusta, and Ellin Greene. *Storytelling: Art and Technique*. 2nd ed. Bowker, 1987.

A revised edition of the popular how-to manual discusses the purpose and value of storytelling and how to select, prepare, and present stories. Additional chapters consider storytelling to children in special settings or with special needs, planning and publicizing story programs, and stories for infants and toddlers.

Bauer, Caroline Feller. *Handbook for Storytellers*. American Library Association, 1977.

An excellent handbook for the beginning or advanced storyteller, this is bursting with ideas for story programs for all ages. The author discusses creative ways to tell stories, including the use of film, music, crafts, puppetry, and magic.

Carlson, Bernice W. *Listen and Help Tell the Story*. Abingdon, 1965.

A book that invites child participation in fingerplays, action verses and stories, and poems or stories with sound effects, refrains, or choruses. Items, which can be used individually or in groups, vary in difficulty, but are best suited to preschoolers or children in the early grades.

Champlin, Connie. *Puppetry and Creative Dramatics in Storytelling*. Renfro Studios, 1980.

Numerous puppet and creative dramatic activities that can be used to extend the delight of popular children's books.

———, and Nancy Renfro. *Storytelling with Puppets*. American Library Association, 1985.

A guide for storytellers who wish to include puppetry in their programs, this includes traditional puppets, finger puppets, cup puppets, shadow puppets, and a myriad of other types that will interest children of all ages.

De Wit, Dorothy. *Children's Faces Looking Up: Program Building for the Storyteller*. American Library Association, 1979.

Especially useful to the beginning storyteller, this includes guidelines for selecting stories, tips for telling, and numerous actual story programs. A complete bibliography is appended.

Irving, Jan, and Robin Currie. *Glad Rags: Stories and Activities Featuring Clothes for Preschool Children*. Libraries Unlimited, 1987.

Includes various ways to share books, games, crafts, and cooking.

———. *Mudluscious: Stories and Activities Featuring Food for Preschool Children*. Libraries Unlimited, 1986.

Similar to the above title, this covers another popular subject in the preschool curriculum.

Livo, Norma, and Sandra J. Rietz. *Storytelling Activities*. Libraries Unlimited, 1987.

Useful for both experienced and inexperienced storytellers, this includes information on finding, designing, and presenting stories.

MacDonald, Margaret R. *Booksharing: 101 Programs to Use with Preschoolers*. Shoe String, 1988.

Complete story programs to use with preschool children. Includes a list of picture books, recordings, and films for each program. An extensive bibliography, including a listing of films, concludes the book.

MacDonald, Margaret R. *Twenty Tellable Tales: Audience Participation for the Beginning Storyteller.* H. W. Wilson, 1986.

Also useful for the practiced storyteller, this collection includes twenty folktales that encourage audience participation.

Nichols, Judy. *Storytimes for Two-Year-Olds.* American Library Association, 1987.

A complete beginner's manual for toddler story times.

Oldfield, Margaret J. *Lots More Tell and Draw Stories.* Creative Storytime, 1973.

————. *More Tell and Draw Stories.* Creative Storytime, 1969.

————. *Tell and Draw Stories.* Creative Storytime. 1963.

These three books demonstrate how to tell original stories while drawing a picture. Most are general animal stories, though *Lots More Tell and Draw Stories* contains some conservation stories.

Peterson, Carolyn S., and Brenny Hall. *Story Programs: A Source Book of Materials.* Scarecrow, 1980.

Sample story programs for toddlers, preschoolers, and primary level children with a bibliography of picture books. Includes detailed instructions for flannel board activities, physical activities, creative dynamics, and puppetry.

Sierra, Judy. *The Flannel Board Storytelling Book.* H. W. Wilson, 1987.

How to make a flannel board and figures and how to use the board to tell stories. Includes eighteen stories, with patterns, for children ages three to five and eighteen stories for children ages five to eight.

Sitarz, Paula G. *Picture Book Story Hours: From Birthdays to Bears.* Libraries Unlimited, 1987.

Twenty-two tested story hour programs to be used as is or as starting points for planning programs for preschoolers.

Tashjian, Virginia. *Juba This and Juba That: Story Hour Stretches for Large or Small Groups.* Little, 1969.

Chants, poetry, fingerplays, riddles, songs, tongue twisters, jokes, and audience participation or action stories to use in story hours.

————. *With a Deep Sea Smile: Story Hour Stretches for Large or Small Groups.* Little, 1974.

Identical in subject to the book listed above, this is another collection of stretches that require audience participation.

Taylor, Frances S., and Gloria G. Vaughn. *The Flannel Board Storybook.* Humanics, 1987.

Patterns for eight "bear" stories, six contemporary stories, seven traditional stories, and four holiday stories to use on the flannel board.

Vonk, Idalee. *Storytelling with the Flannel Board*. Book 3, Denison, 1983.
Original stories and folktales with flannel board illustrations, similar to
Paul Anderson's books, above.

Warren, Jean. *Cut and Tell Scissor Stories for Fall*. Warren, 1984.

——. *Cut and Tell Scissor Stories for Spring*. Warren, 1984.

——. *Cut and Tell Scissor Stories for Winter*. Warren, 1984.
All three books contain original seasonal stories designed to be told
while cutting out patterns on a paper plate. Additional activities are included at the end of each story.

5. Gift Books for Young Children

SUE McCLEAF-NESPECA

INTENDED AUDIENCE: Parents, grandparents, and other potential gift-givers

LENGTH: One hour

SUMMARY OF PROGRAM: The purpose of this program is to interest adults in giving books for holidays and other special occasions and to discuss how to choose books for young children. The talk emphasizes the importance of building a home library and encourages adults to give children good literature, beginning at birth.

HINTS FOR PLANNING AND PRESENTATION: Read aloud or tell the stories from several books that you feel would make good gifts for children. Briefly discuss another twenty or thirty titles, pointing out those appropriate for children at certain ages. Be sure that every title you discuss is currently in print. Display as many titles as possible; try to have multiple copies available so participants can take books home for further examination. Allow plenty of time for questions and browsing.

This is an ideal program to hold early in November (possibly during Children's Book Week) so participants have enough time to purchase books for the holidays.

I. INTRODUCTION

A. Tell why you believe books make perfect gifts for children.
1. Books, unlike toys, do not break or need batteries, and they can be kept a lifetime.
2. Books are important to a child's learning experience during the crucial early years. A gift of a book can contribute to a child's educational experience.
3. Books are portable and can be enjoyed while traveling or waiting in lines or at offices.
4. Children who learn to enjoy books at an early age often become early readers.

70

B. Suggest that books are good gifts not only for Hanukkah or Christmas, but also for birthdays or other special occasions.

    1. Include a book in your child's Easter basket.

    2. Send a favorite book as a special valentine.

II. HOW TO CHOOSE BOOKS FOR CHILDREN

A. Explain the importance of picking quality literature. Read or tell some picture book stories: *Corduroy, Ask Mr. Bear,* or *Harry the Dirty Dog.* Stress these points:

    1. Quality literature is not didactic, biased, or written just for the message alone.

    2. Quote Margaret Mary Kimmel in *For Reading Out Loud!*: "Outstanding literature shapes and communicates the human experience in such a way as to illuminate, move, or delight the listener."[1]

    3. Children are entitled to literature written in a way that does not talk down to them or treat them as inferior.

    4. Children deserve books that are not dull. Children who are exposed to quality literature will learn what quality literature is.

    5. Exposure to the rich language of good literature enhances the development of a child's speaking language.

B. Emphasize the importance of choosing books with good illustrations. Show several examples of fine picture book art: *The Three Billy Goats Gruff* by Paul Galdone, *One Hunter, Freight Train, Where the Wild Things Are.* Stress these points:

    1. This is a child's first introduction to art, and it may be the only real art that a child sees for some time.

    2. Sharing books with good illustrations teaches the child, by example, what constitutes good art.

    3. A child's visual imagination is stimulated by finely illustrated picture books.

    4. The illustrations and text of a good picture book are of equal importance. The illustrations enhance and extend the story and contribute to the child's understanding of the text.

C. Talk about how picture books are more innovative than in the past, stimulating a child's imagination with flaps, holes, raised-relief surfaces to touch and feel, and size. Show several examples: *The Very*

---

1. Mary Margaret Kimmel and Elizabeth Segel, *For Reading Out Loud! A Guide to Sharing Books with Children,* rev. ed. (New York: Delacorte, 1988).

Busy Spider and *The Very Hungry Caterpillar*; *Where's Spot?*; *Pat the Bunny*; *Nutshell Library*.

D. Encourage participants to choose books that appeal to them. Suggest that they look at the actual bookmaking and make sure bindings are durable.

E. Show a few of the many guides written to help adults select books for children, for example, *Choosing Books for Children*[2] by Betsy Hearne and *Good Books to Grow On*[3] by Andrea E. Cascardi.

III. BUILDING A HOME LIBRARY

A. Discuss how important it is to establish a home library from the time of the child's birth.
   1. Quote Aidan Chambers in *Introducing Books to Children*: "Readers are made, not born."[4]
   2. Establish a certain place for the child's library.
   3. Place books within the child's reach. Be sure that they are low enough for the child to grab at any time of the day, but high enough to discourage pets.

B. Give examples of good baby gifts, "first books for baby's shelf":
   1. *The Baby's Lap Book* or *The Baby's Storybook*
   2. *Eye Winker, Tom Tinker, Chin Chopper*
   3. The *Helen Oxenbury Nursery Story Book*
   4. *All Asleep*
   5. *The Real Mother Goose*
   6. *One, Two, Three and What Is It?*

C. Talk about where participants may purchase children's books.
   1. Bookstores. Be sure to point out that bookstores can order any book in print. Show *Children's Books in Print*.[5]
   2. Attending library book sales can sometimes be profitable.
   3. Quality books can be bought occasionally at garage sales, second-hand bookstores and thrift shops.

2. Betsy Hearne, *Choosing Books for Children: A Common Sense Guide* (New York: Delacorte, 1981).

3. Andrea E. Cascardi, *Good Books to Grow On: A Guide to Building Your Child's Library from Birth to Age Five* (New York: Warner, 1985).

4. Aidan Chambers, *Introducing Books to Children*, 2nd ed. (Boston: Horn Book, 1983).

5. *Children's Books in Print, 1988–1989: An Author, Title, and Illustrator Index to Children's Books* (New York: Bowker, 1988).

D. Stress the importance of teaching young children to respect books and handle them with care.

1. Do not write or color in books.

2. Do not sit or step on books.

3. Do not leave books outdoors.

4. These habits, taught early, will help the child use library books properly.

Thirty-five Gift Books That Can't Miss

Brown, Margaret Wise. *Goodnight, Moon*. Illus. by Clement Hurd. Harper, 1947.

Carle, Eric. *The Very Busy Spider*. Putnam, 1984.

―――. *The Very Hungry Caterpillar*. Putnam, 1981.

Chorao, Kay. *The Baby's Lap Book*. Dutton, 1977.

―――. *The Baby's Story Book*. Dutton, 1985.

Crews, Donald. *Freight Train*. Greenwillow, 1978.

De Brunhoff, Jean, and Laurent De Brunhoff. *Babar's Anniversary Album*. Random, 1981.

dePaola, Tomie, illus. *Tomie dePaola's Mother Goose*. Putnam, 1985.

Flack, Marjorie. *Ask Mr. Bear*. Macmillan, 1932.

Freeman, Donald. *Corduroy*. Viking, 1968.

Gag, Wanda. *Millions of Cats*. Putnam, 1977.

Galdone, Paul. *The Three Billy Goats Gruff*. Houghton Mifflin, 1973.

Glazer, Tom. *Eye Winker, Tom Tinker, Chin Chopper: Fifty Musical Fingerplays*. Doubleday, 1973.

Hill, Eric. *Where's Spot?* Putnam, 1980.

Hoban, Tana. *One, Two, Three*. Greenwillow, 1985.

―――. *What Is It?* Greenwillow, 1985.

Hutchins, Pat. *One Hunter*. Greenwillow, 1982.

Kennedy, Jimmy. *The Teddy Bears' Picnic*. Illus. by Alexandra Day. Green Tiger Press, 1983.

Kunhardt, Dorothy. *Pat the Bunny*. Western, 1942.

Lobel, Arnold. *On Market Street*. Illus. by Anita Lobel. Greenwillow, 1981.

Marshall, James. *Goldilocks and the Three Bears*. Dial, 1988.

Martin, Bill. *Brown Bear, Brown Bear, What Do You See?* Illus. by Eric Carle. Holt, 1983.

Matthiesen, Thomas. *ABC: An Alphabet Book*. Putnam, 1981.

Milne, A. A. *Pooh's Bedtime Book*. Dutton, 1980.

Oxenbury, Helen. *The Helen Oxenbury Nursery Story Book*. Knopf, 1985.

Pomerantz, Charlotte. *All Asleep*. Illus. by Nancy Tafuri. Greenwillow, 1984.

Potter, Beatrix. *The Tale of Peter Rabbit*. Warne, 1902.

Read Aloud Rhymes for the Very Young. Ed. by Jack Prelutsky. Illus. by Marc Brown. Knopf, 1986.

Rey, H. A. *Curious George*. Houghton Mifflin, 1941.

Rockwell, Anne. *The Three Bears and Fifteen Other Stories*. Crowell, 1975.

Sendak, Maurice. *Nutshell Library*. Harper, 1962. (Boxed set)

――――. *Where the Wild Things Are*. Harper, 1963.

Steig, William. *Doctor DeSoto*. Farrar, 1982.

Wright, Blanche, illus. *The Real Mother Goose*. Macmillan, 1987.

Zion, Gene. *Harry the Dirty Dog*. Harper, 1956.

6. Power of Books: Using Literature in the Religious Education of Young Children

MARALITA L. FREENY

INTENDED AUDIENCE: Religious educators, for example, parents and teachers in religious education programs

LENGTH: Approximately forty-five minutes

SUMMARY OF PROGRAM: This program presents an introduction to picture books for parents and teachers involved in religious and ethical education of children. It outlines the general benefits of reading aloud, the power of books, and presents examples of picture books suitable for teaching values, for promoting positive emotional development, for introducing the Bible and for assisting in the solving of childhood problems. It closes with a presentation of other library resources available to parents, including adult books about morality and ethics among children and bibliographic tools pertaining to children's books.

HINTS FOR PLANNING AND PRESENTATION: Be sure to display as many of the picture books as you can so that participants can see them and handle them at the end of the program. Leave time for browsing among the books and, of course, for questions and answers. Have a copy of *A to Zoo*,[1] *Growing Pains*,[2] or *Bookfinder*[3] to help you in case a book title doesn't come to mind immediately when you are answering questions. Above all, choose only books that you can present enthusiastically in the core of your presentation, and let your enthusiasm show.

---

1. Carolyn W. Lima and John A. Lima, *A to Zoo: Subject Access to Children's Picture Books*, 3rd ed. (New York: Bowker, 1989).

2. Maureen Cuddigan and Mary Beth Hanson, *Growing Pains: Helping Children Deal with Everyday Problems through Reading* (Chicago: American Library Association, 1988).

3. Sharon Spredemann Dreyer, *Bookfinder: A Guide to Children's Literature about the Needs and Problems of Youth Aged 2–15* (New York: American Guidance Service, 1977).

I. INTRODUCTION

   A. Tell about my background in the children's library field.

   B. Present purpose of the program.

      1. To outline the benefits of reading aloud.

      2. To present picture books suitable for use in the religious upbringing and ethical education of young children.

      3. To present adult books and children's bibliographic tools to use in the religious upbringing of children.

II. VALUE OF READING ALOUD: THE POWER OF BOOKS

   A. Development of reading readiness skills.

   B. Enhancement of language development.

   C. Reinforcement of values of education and positive emotional development.

   D. Development of problem-solving relationship between parent and child.

   E. Pure enjoyment.

III. FOSTERING VALUES AND POSITIVE EMOTIONAL DEVELOPMENT THROUGH CHILDREN'S BOOKS

   The use of good literature facilitates the teaching of values. A well-written picture book presents the desired qualities or values within a context understandable by young children. Both the rewards of good behavior and the consequences of inappropriate behavior are illustrated in the books cited in this section. Additionally, books which foster positive emotional development, such as the formation of a good self-concept, are introduced.

   A. Positive self-concept. Present stories in which the main characters are presented in positive terms in spite of shortcomings or differences.

      The value of being oneself is promoted in *Dandelion, Wizard of Wallaby Wallow*, and *Circus Baby*.

      Ton and Pon in *Ton and Pon: Big and Little* demonstrate the advantages of being different from others.

   B. Knowing one's abilities; accepting one's limitations. Books can show children that they may not always know their own capabilities. After locking himself in the house, Alfie learns that he can free himself through his own resources in *Alfie Gets In First*.

      Children can learn from a well-written picture book that they needn't always be perfect and that their abilities may not be the same as those of other people. The chicken in *The Chick and the Duckling* learns from his mistakes that he cannot swim like the duckling.

C. Developing personal values. Picture books provide an excellent jumping-off point for a parent and child discussion of appropriate and inappropriate behavior and of personal values, such as truth, integrity, and loyalty.

    A Great Big Enormous Lie and *Molly's Lie* deal with lying and emphasize the value of telling the truth.

    Traditional folktales often promote positive values. In *The Greedy Shopkeeper*, a Yugoslavian tale, a poor farmer's integrity and honesty win him a big reward.

D. Expressing feelings. In their preschool years, children need to learn that the feelings they are experiencing, both positive and negative, are normal. Picture book stories which treat emotions in a non-didactic way reinforce the notion that feelings are shared by others and that they are perfectly normal.

    Feelings by Aliki might lead children to an open discussion of their emotions.

    Fear is common among young children. *Holes and Peeks* addresses the fear of scary holes, such as the toiletbowl or the bathtub drain. Fear of monsters is treated cleverly in *Clyde Monster*, in which a young monster is afraid of people. Picture books can be found on a variety of fears—the dark, spiders, dogs, and bullies, for example.

    Read about jealousy in *The Pain and the Great One*, about envy in *I Wish I Was Sick Too!* and *It's Not Fair*, and about anger in *The Hating Book*.

    Picture books are available on other emotions as well, such as love, embarrassment, generosity, loneliness, happiness, sadness. Refer to *Growing Pains* or *A to Zoo* for recommendations of specific titles.

E. Family relationships. Many excellent books are available on the problems of family life, but they are treated in other parts of this presentation. The books outlined here deal with a child's relationship to the various members of the family.

    All Kinds of Families explains the concept of family and introduces the various members of a family.

    The parent and child relationship is described in *Just Me and My Dad* and *Claude and Pepper*.

    In *Tell Me Grandma, Tell Me Grandpa*, a child learns what her parents were like when they were small. The book capably depicts the child's relationship to her grandparents, as well as the grandparents' relationships to the child's parents.

The special relationship shared by children and their grandparents is described in *Georgia Music*.

Sibling relationships are treated in a positive way in *We're Very Good Friends, My Brother and I* and *101 Things to Do with a Baby*.

F. Friendship. Many aspects of friendship are dealt with in picture books. Rivalry, jealousy, and envy are among the conflicts treated. The absence of friends, the development of new friendships, and the true meaning of friendship are other aspects covered in the many books on friends.

Katharine's Doll, The Wizard, the Fairy and the Magic Chicken, and *Mine's the Best* deal with friendships in conflict.

School is the setting for two excellent books on making friends, *Timothy Goes to School* and *Will I Have a Friend?*

G. Accepting other cultures. An understanding of other cultures can be fostered through the reading of a well-written book.

People presents an overview of the differences among cultures throughout the world.

Africa is the setting for *Jafta's Mother, Not So Fast, Songololo*, and *The Village of Round and Square Houses*.

How My Parents Learned to Eat introduces the concept that even eating habits vary from culture to culture.

IV. USING CHILDREN'S BOOKS AS TOOLS FOR COPING WITH AND SOLVING PROBLEMS

Children encounter numerous stressful situations during their preschool years, and parents have at their disposal a variety of means to help them assist their children in coping with problems. Bibliotherapy is an effective method of defining a problem and setting about to solve it. The reading of a good book can lead the parent and child to an open discussion of problems; it can also show children that their problems are not unique.

A. Toilet training. Toilet training can be a very stressful time in a toddler's life. Picture books can assist a parent in preparing a child for this important developmental step.

No More Diapers is a dual-purpose book that has one section for girls, another for boys.

Going to the Potty, illustrated with photographs, presents toilet training in a direct, encouraging way.

B. School and day care. Going to school or day care for the first time can be a frightening experience for a child. Books that introduce the activities a child might experience and describe the setting and people they might expect to encounter can help alleviate some of the fear.

Fred Rogers, a master of reassuring children, has written *Going to Day Care* in order to prepare children for their first experiences in a day care setting.

Nursery school is the subject of *My Nursery School* and *Shawn Goes to School*. *Starting School, I Don't Want to Go to School*, and *When You Go to Kindergarten* were written to provide reassurance to a child who is starting kindergarten or first grade.

C. New baby and sibling rivalry. There are numerous books available to help prepare children for a new baby and to help them deal with their intense jealousy after the arrival of the new sibling.

The subject of jealousy of a new baby is approached humorously in *The Very Worst Monster* and *Nobody Asked Me If I Wanted a Baby Sister*.

It's a Baby!, which describes what it's like to have a baby around the house, would be useful in preparing a child for a sibling's birth. *Waiting for Jennifer* describes the long wait for a new baby.

When Peter realizes that he's too big for his old chair, he consents to painting it pink for his little sister Susie. *Peter's Chair* presents the sibling relationship in a positive light.

D. Moving. Moving can be a threatening and frightening experience for a young child. Whether it is the child himself, a friend, or family member who is moving away, the experience can fill a child with anxiety.

Moving and *Bears' Moving Day* will help prepare a child whose family is moving.

Mitchell Is Moving, and *We Are Best Friends* deal with children whose best friends are moving away.

E. Death of a pet. Coping with death is difficult at any age, but particularly so for small children who have little or no understanding of death.

Books about the death of a pet can be especially useful when a child experiences such a loss, but they can also be used to elicit discussion about death in general.

Accident and *Jim's Dog Muffins* both deal effectively with the grieving process. The main character in each book experiences the death of a pet dog.

A child's coping with the death of a pet cat is the subject of *The Tenth Good Thing about Barney*.

F. Thumbsucking and security objects. It is not unusual for a parent or caregiver to deal inappropriately with a child's dependence on thumbsucking or security objects, such as blankets and teddy bears. In these cases, a good picture book can be as instructive to the adult as it is reassuring to the child.

The subtitle of *David Decides about Thumbsucking: A Motivating Story for Children: An Informative Guide for Parents*, sums up its usefulness.

The Blanket That Had to Go and *Bye Bye, Old Buddy* address the conflict children experience when they feel they must give up a security object. *Ira Sleeps Over* is a reassuring story about a boy's need for his teddy bear at bedtime. In the story, Ira, who sleeps with a teddy, is relieved to learn that his friend Reggie does too.

G. Babysitters and separation anxiety. Even a short-term separation from one's parents can be stressful for young children. Books about babysitters and separation anxiety can help prepare a child for such an experience.

The Berenstain Bears and the Sitter is just one of many books by Stan and Jan Berenstain written to help children cope with difficult situations.

You Go Away presents various situations in which children are separated from their parents.

In *Bear and Mrs. Duck*, Bear's reluctance to stay with the babysitter, Mrs. Duck, is typical of young bears who act as children do. Children may see themselves in Bear, and reading about Bear's experiences with Mrs. Duck may better prepare them for their own babysitters.

V. INTRODUCING THE BIBLE AND PRAYERS

Introduction of the Bible and praying is essential in the religious upbringing of children. Many high-quality books that chronicle Bible stories and present prayers and spiritual poetry are now available on a child's level.

A. Bible stories. Collections of Bible stories are good choices for home use, especially nicely illustrated ones such as *Brian Wildsmith's Illustrated Bible Stories*. Like the former title, *A First Bible* and *Bible Stories for Children* are collections written and illustrated specifically for youngsters.

Many popular Bible stories are published in individual, illustrated versions. These provide additional details about the chosen stories through longer texts and more illustrations. *Noah and the Ark*, *A Child Is Born*, *Joseph and His Brothers*, and *Jonah and the Great Fish* are just four of the many individual Bible stories now available. These would be especially appropriate for sharing with a Sunday school class.

B. Books of prayers. Books of prayers provide good reading for families, especially at bedtime, a traditional time for praying.

The books mentioned here contain prayers and inspirational poetry written on a child's level; they also feature illustrations that will appeal to preschoolers and adults alike.

Prayer for a Child is an original prayer by Rachel Field. Two popular illustrators have compiled and illustrated favorite prayers and poems in *A Child's Book of Prayers* by Michael Hague and *First Prayers* by Tasha Tudor.

VI. USING OTHER RESOURCES FOR THE TEACHING OF RELIGION AND MORALITY

A. Adult books about morality and ethics in children. Parents and educators have at their disposal a number of resources to assist them in the religious and moral upbringing of their children. I will mention them only by title; an annotated resource list that outlines the uses of each of the books is available to you.

1. *Smart Times*
2. *Moral Life of Children*
3. *Moral Development*
4. *The Complete Book of Baby and Child Care for Christian Parents*
5. *Raising Good Children*
6. *Teaching Your Child to Make Decisions*
7. *Helping Your Child Learn Right from Wrong*
8. *Peace in the Family*
9. *Parenting for Peace and Justice*

B. Bibliographic tools. This talk has introduced you to just a small selection of the many picture books available on topics pertinent to the religious and moral upbringing of children. Refer to the following tools for additional suggestions.

1. *A to Zoo: Subject Access to Children's Picture Books*
2. *Bookfinder*
3. *Growing Pains: Helping Children Deal with Everyday Problems through Reading*

A Booklist

Positive Self-Concept

Carlson, Nancy. *Harriet's Recital*. Carolrhoda, 1982.
Freeman, Don. *Dandelion*. Viking, 1964.
Iwamura, Kazuo. *Ton and Pon: Big and Little*. Bradbury, 1984.
Kent, Jack. *Wizard of Wallaby Wallow*. Parents, 1971.
Petersham, Maud, and Miska Petersham. *Circus Baby*. Macmillan, 1968.

Knowing One's Abilities; Accepting One's Limitations

Aruego, José. *Look What I Can Do*. Scribner, 1971.
Ginsburg, Mirra. *The Chick and the Duckling*. Illus. by José Aruego and Ariane Dewey. Macmillan, 1972.
Hughes, Shirley. *Alfie Gets In First*. Lothrop, 1972.
Kraus, Robert. *Leo the Late Bloomer*. Crowell, 1971.

Developing Personal Values

Berenstain, Stan, and Jan Berenstain. *Berenstain Bears and the Truth*. Random, 1983.
Chorao, Kay. *Molly's Lie*. Seabury, 1979.
Hazen, Barbara S. *The Gorilla Did It*. Illus. by Ray Cruz. Atheneum, 1974.
Lionni, Leo. *Frederick*. Pantheon, 1966.
Mirkovic, Irene. *The Greedy Shopkeeper*. Illus. by Harold Berson. Harcourt, 1980.
Sharmat, Marjorie W. *A Big Fat Enormous Lie*. Dutton, 1978.
Williams, Barbara. *Albert's Toothache*. Illus. by Kay Chorao. Dutton, 1974.

Expressing Feelings

Aliki. *Feelings*. Greenwillow, 1984.
Blume, Judy. *The Pain and the Great One*. Illus. by Irene Trivas. Bradbury, 1984.
Brandenberg, Franz. *I Wish I Was Sick Too!* Illus. by Aliki. Greenwillow, 1976.
Crowe, Robert. *Clyde Monster*. Illus. by Kay Chorao. Dutton, 1976.
DuBois, William P. *Bear Party*. Penguin, 1987.
Jonas, Ann. *Holes and Peeks*. Greenwillow, 1984.
Zolotow, Charlotte. *The Hating Book*. Harper, 1969.

Family Relationships

Gackenback, Dick. *Claude and Pepper*. Houghton Mifflin, 1976.

Griffith, Helen. *Georgia Music*. Illus. by James Stevenson. Greenwillow, 1986.

Hallinan, P. K. *We're Very Good Friends, My Brother and I*. Childrens Press, 1973.

Mayer, Mercer. *Just Me and My Dad*. Western, 1977.

Newman, Shirlee. *Tell Me Grandma, Tell Me Grandpa*. Houghton Mifflin, 1979.

Ormerod, Jan. *101 Things to Do with a Baby*. Lothrop, 1984.

Simon, Norma. *All Kinds of Families*. Illus. by Joe Lasker. Whitman, 1975.

Friendship

Bonsall, Crosby. *Mine's the Best*. Harper, 1973.

Cohen, Miriam. *Will I Have a Friend?* Macmillan, 1967.

Kellogg, Steven. *Won't Somebody Play with Me?* Dial, 1972.

Lester, Helen. *The Wizard, the Fairy and the Magic Chicken*. Illus. by Lynn Munsinger. Houghton Mifflin, 1983.

Wells, Rosemary. *Timothy Goes to School*. Dial, 1981.

Winthrop, Elizabeth. *Katharine's Doll*. Illus. by Marilyn Hafner. Dutton, 1983.

Accepting Other Cultures

Daly, Niki. *Not So Fast, Songololo*. Atheneum, 1986.

Friedman, Ina. *How My Parents Learned to Eat*. Illus. by Allen Say. Houghton Mifflin, 1984.

Grifalconi, Ann. *The Village of Round and Square Houses*. Little, 1986.

Lewin, Hugh. *Jafta's Mother*. Illus. by Lisa Kopper. Carolrhoda, 1983.

Spier, Peter. *People*. Doubleday, 1980.

Toilet Training

Brooks, Joae G. *No More Diapers*. Dell, 1982.

Rogers, Fred. *Going to the Potty*. Putnam, 1986.

School and Day Care

Bram, Elizabeth. *I Don't Want to Go to School*. Greenwillow, 1977.

Breinburg, Petronella. *Shawn Goes to School*. Illus. by Errol Lloyd. Crowell, 1974.

Howe, James. *When You Go to Kindergarten*. Knopf, 1986.

Rockwell, Harlow. *My Nursery School*. Greenwillow, 1976.

Rogers, Fred. *Going to Day Care*. Putnam, 1985.

Stanek, Muriel. *Starting School*. Illus. by Tony and Betty De Luna. Whitman, 1981.

New Baby and Siblings

Alexander, Martha. *Nobody Asked Me If I Wanted a Baby Sister*. Dial, 1971.

Ancona, George. *It's a Baby!* Dutton, 1979.

Galbraith, Kathryn O. *Waiting for Jennifer*. Illus. by Irene Trivas. Macmillan, 1987.

Hutchins, Pat. *The Very Worst Monster*. Greenwillow, 1985.

Keats, Ezra Jack. *Peter's Chair*. Harper, 1967.

Moving

Aliki. *We Are Best Friends*. Greenwillow, 1982.

Gretz, Susanna. *Teddy Bears' Moving Day*. Macmillan, 1981.

Rogers, Fred. *Moving*. Putnam, 1987.

Sharmat, Marjorie W. *Mitchell Is Moving*. Illus. by José Aruego and Ariane Dewey. Macmillan, 1985.

Death of a Pet

Carrick, Carol. *Accident*. Illus. by Donald Carrick. Houghton Mifflin, 1976.

Cohen, Miriam. *Jim's Dog Muffins*. Greenwillow, 1984.

Viorst, Judith. *The Tenth Good Thing about Barney*. Illus. by Eric Blegvac. Atheneum, 1971.

Thumbsucking and Security Objects

Cooney, Nancy E. *The Blanket That Had to Go*. Putnam, 1981.

Heitler, Susan M. *David Decides about Thumbsucking*. Illus. by Paula Singer. Reading Matters, 1985.

Robison, Deborah. *Bye Bye, Old Buddy*. Houghton Mifflin, 1983.

Waber, Bernard. *Ira Sleeps Over*. Houghton Mifflin, 1972.

Babysitters and Separation Anxiety

Berenstain, Stan, and Jan Berenstain. *Berenstain Bears and the Sitter*. Random, 1981.

Corey, Dorothy. *You Go Away*. Illus. by Caroline Rubin and Lois Axeman. Whitman, 1975.

Hughes, Shirley. *Alfie Gives a Hand*. Lothrop, 1984.

Winthrop, Elizabeth. *Bear and Mrs. Duck*. Illus. by Patience Brewster. Holiday, 1988.

Collections of Bible Stories

A First Bible. Illus. by Helen Sewell. Walck, 1958.

Horn, Geoffrey. *Bible Stories for Children*. Macmillan, 1980.

Marshall, Catherine. *Catherine Marshall's Story Bible*. Avon, 1982.

Turner, Philip. *Brian Wildsmith's Illustrated Bible Stories*. Illus. by Brian Wildsmith. Watts, 1968.

Individual Bible Stories

dePaola, Tomie. *Noah and the Ark*. Winston, 1983.
Kindvall, Ella K. *Jonah and the Great Fish*. Moody, 1984.
Steele, Philip. *Joseph and His Brothers*. Silver, 1985.
Winthrop, Elizabeth. *A Child Is Born: The Christmas Story*. Holiday, 1983.

Books of Prayers

Field, Rachel. *Prayer for a Child*. Macmillan, 1984.
Hague, Michael. *A Child's Book of Prayers*. Holt, 1985.
Tudor, Tasha. *First Prayers*. McKay, 1962.

A Resource List for Teaching Morality and Ethics to Children

Burtt, Kent Garland. *Smart Times: A Parent's Guide to Quality Time with Preschoolers*. Harper, 1984.
   Selecting examples that are not only entertaining for kids but also pleasurable for parents, Burtt describes games designed to promote the child's physical, social, and cognitive skills. Two chapters helpful in fostering the moral development of youngsters are "Communicating Feelings" and "Sharing Social, Moral and Spiritual Values."
Coles, Robert. *Moral Life of Children*. Atlantic Monthly Press, 1986.
   A child psychiatrist approaches the study of the moral thinking of children through direct observation; he examines children of varying origins and ages who face every kind of moral challenge.
Dorn, Lois. *Peace in the Family*. Pantheon, 1983.
   With a broad array of exercises, practical programs, and sound examples, Dorn outlines a course of action to help parents establish effective two-way communication between generations.
Duska, Ronald. *Moral Development: A Guide to Piaget and Kohlberg*. Paulist Press, 1975.
   Duska presents theories of moral development that, according to their proponents, clearly show the stages an individual goes through in achieving moral maturity, relates their relevance to Christian moral development, and looks at their impact on Christian morality.
Ketterman, Grace H., and Herbert L. Ketterman. *The Complete Book of Baby and Child Care for Christian Parents*. Fleming H. Revell, 1982.
   A child-care manual written within a Christian context. Suggests ways to

help parents raise children to become caring, responsible, and spiritually committed adults.

Lickona, Thomas. *Raising Good Children: From Birth through the Teenage Years.* Bantam, 1983.

Lickona describes the predictable stages of moral development from infancy to adulthood and offers practical advice and guidance for each stage.

McGinnis, Kathleen, and James McGinnis. *Parenting for Peace and Justice.* Orbis, 1982.

Staff members of the Institute for Peace and Justice, the McGinnises have written concrete guidelines for involving the family in social action. Chapters, dealing with such topics as materialism, violence, racism, and sex-role stereotyping, explore a dimension of the integration of social and family ministry.

Miller, Gordon Porter. *Teaching Your Child to Make Decisions: How to Raise a Responsible Child.* Harper, 1984.

Dr. Miller shows how to apply standard decision making techniques to help children learn to make choices.

Simon, Sidney B., and Sally Wendhos Olds. *Helping Your Child Learn Right from Wrong: A Guide to Values Clarification.* Simon and Schuster, 1976.

Simon and Olds provide parents with a practical system for helping their children learn right from wrong through values clarification. Based on an assortment of strategies, the process helps families examine their feelings about love, friendship, money, work, honesty, and responsibility.

7. Finding Picture Books for Special Needs

HARRIET HERSCHEL

INTENDED AUDIENCE: Adults who are not trained as children's librarians but are working with children in the public library

LENGTH: Forty-five minutes to one hour

SUMMARY OF PROGRAM: This is one section of an in-service training workshop on picture books. The purpose of the program is to show the variety of picture books on special needs and introduce briefly the role of bibliotherapy.

HINTS FOR PLANNING AND PRESENTATION: Background reading of picture books as well as a review of some professional resources for finding picture books on special needs will be necessary. *Problems of Early Childhood: An Annotated Guide*, by Elizabeth Hirsch, is particularly helpful for understanding the difficulties of childhood.[1] The problems covered include such experiences as hospitalization, the death of beloved persons, divorce, single parenting, mothers going to work, a new baby in the family, and going to school. *Books to Help Children Cope with Separation and Loss*, by Joanne E. Bernstein, is also a helpful overview, which lists books for older children as well.[2] It includes a good introductory chapter on the role of bibliotherapy.

When presenting the program, booktalk or read as many picture books as possible. Demonstrate how professional resources are useful in identifying books on special subjects. Allow time for viewing book displays, asking questions, handing out booklists, and evaluating the program.

---

1. Elizabeth Hirsch, *Problems of Early Childhood: An Annotated Guide* (New York: Garland, 1983).
2. Joanne E. Bernstein, *Books to Help Children Cope with Separation and Loss* (New York: Bowker, 1977).

I. INTRODUCTION

A. Define bibliotherapy. Bibliotherapy is a means of helping a person cope with a problem through the use of books.

B. Present the values of bibliotherapy.

1. Using books can be an effective way to help both parents and children understand problems and concerns.

2. The use of books written on a child's level can help a parent verbalize a problem with the child.

3. Bibliotherapy is a means of helping children realize that they are not alone and that many other children share the problem.

4. The use of books may serve as a catharsis for children.

C. Explain the scope of the presentation. I have tried to cover books on the more commonly requested subjects, such as the birth of a new sibling, divorce and the single parent, going to the doctor and the hospital experience, death and dying, and books that reflect special children and their situations. Since I have included books on the whole life cycle, from birth to death, I will discuss the books in that order.

II. NEW BABY AND SIBLING RIVALRY

Having a new sibling in the family is a major change for a young child. The child experiences many emotions—anger, fear, guilt, depression, and jealousy—some of them for the first time. Read or booktalk a variety of the following titles:

Alexander, Martha G. *Nobody Asked Me If I Wanted a Baby Sister*. Dial, 1971.
A little boy tries to give his baby sister away until he discovers he is the only one who can comfort her.

Ancona, George. *It's a Baby!* Dutton, 1979.
Photographs and simple text explain a baby's development from birth to his first birthday.

Berger, Terry. *A New Baby*. Childrens Press, 1974.
A young boy wonders what the new baby will be like and whether his parents will still love him.

Edelman, Elaine. *I Love My Baby Sister (Most of the Time)*. Lothrop, 1984.
Humorous illustrations depict the mixed blessings of a new baby from a child's point of view.

Greenfield, Eloise. *She Come Bringing Me That Little Baby Girl*. Illus. by John Steptoe. Lippincott, 1974.
A boy wishes for a baby brother but gets a sister instead. After

initially feeling resentful of the attention paid to her, he realizes that he is proud of his new sister.

Hamilton, Morse and Emily. *My Name Is Emily*. Greenwillow, 1979.
Emily has just returned from running away, and her father pretends not to recognize her. From this pretend game, Emily resolves her jealousy of a new baby.

Hoban, Russell. *A Baby Sister for Frances*. Harper, 1976.
Frances runs away from home when she thinks baby sister Gloria is getting too much attention. She returns when she overhears her parents saying how much they miss her.

Jarrell, Mary. *Knee Baby*. Illus. by Symeon Shimin. Farrar, 1973.
Alan feels displaced by his baby sister until Mother takes the time to make him feel loved.

Keats, Ezra Jack. *Peter's Chair*. Harper, 1967.
Peter feels resentful when his little sister takes over his crib and cradle, so he decides to run away and take his little chair with him. When the chair turns out to be too small for him, he returns and helps paint it pink for Susie.

Lindgren, Astrid. *I Want a Brother or Sister*. Illus. by Ilon Wikland. Harper, 1981.
When a newborn arrives at Peter's house, he discovers that maybe he didn't really want a brother or sister after all. Through Mother's comfort and understanding, Peter starts to enjoy and feel proud of his baby sister.

Ormerod, Jan. *101 Things to Do with a Baby*. Lothrop, 1984.
From morning to bedtime, a little girl and her baby brother do 101 things together, often with their parents' assistance. A warm and reassuring look at sibling relationships.

Relf, Patricia. *That New Baby*. Golden, 1980.
Having a new baby in the house can be very upsetting for an older brother or sister.

Rogers, Fred. *New Baby*. Putnam, 1985.
Fred Rogers writes about the feelings an older child may experience when a new baby is introduced to a household. Color photographs of realistic family situations accompany the text.

Scott, Ann. *On Mother's Lap*. Illus. by Glo Coalson. McGraw, 1972.
A mother reassures her little boy, who claims the baby won't fit on her lap. There is always room for both of them.

Stein, Sara Bonnett. *That New Baby: An Open Family Book for Parents and Children Together*. Walker, 1974.
An explanation of children's feelings about a new baby, written for parents, accompanies a text for children, with lots of photographs.

Walter, Mildred Pitts. *My Mamma Needs Me*. Illus. by Pat Cummings. Lothrop, 1983.
A little boy feels displaced by a new baby until he realizes how much his mother needs him.

Wells, Rosemary. *Noisy Nora*. Dial, 1973.
When Mother's attentions are focused on the new baby Nora becomes very noisy lest the family forget about her.

III. ADOPTION

There are not a lot of high-quality picture books about adoption for the young child. I would booktalk *Chosen Baby* and *Being Adopted*, both of which show multi-ethnic families.

Bunin, Catherine. *Is That Your Sister? A True Story of Adoption*. Pantheon, 1976.
Catherine, a six-year-old girl, tells what it is like to be adopted into a multi-racial family.

Caines, Jeannette Franklin. *Abby*. Illus. by Steven Kellogg. Harper, 1973.
A preschool child asks her mother about adoption.

Milgram, Mary. *Brothers Are All the Same*. Dutton, 1978.
A neighbor boy wonders how Joshie can be a brother to his friends Nina and Kim when his skin color is so much darker than theirs.

Rosenberg, Maxine. *Being Adopted*. Photos by George Ancona. Lothrop, 1984.
Several young children recount their experiences of being adopted. All have racial and cultural roots different from those of their adoptive families.

Wasson, Valentina P. *Chosen Baby*. Lippincott, 1977.
Originally published in 1939, this up-dated story explains the process of adoption and how the Brown family came to be a family.

IV. GOING TO THE DOCTOR AND THE HOSPITAL EXPERIENCE

Going to the doctor or hospital can be a traumatic experience for a young child. There are many good books to help a child deal with this situation. Be sure to introduce one of the titles that is illustrated with photographs and explain how familiarity with the doctor's tools or the hospital's environment can prepare a child better for a new or frightening experience.

Bemelmans, Ludwig. *Madeline*. Penguin, 1977.
In this classic story, children learn about Madeline's emergency operation.

Bruna, Dick. *Miffy in the Hospital*. Methuen, 1975.
A simple story about a hospital experience, appropriate for a very young child.

DeSantis, Kenny. *Doctors' Tools*. Dodd, 1985.
Useful explanation of some of the instruments commonly used in a doctor's office.

Krementz, Jill. *Taryn Goes to the Dentist*. Crown, 1986.
A board book that explains what to expect when visiting the dentist.

Marino, Barbara. *Eric Needs Stitches*. Illus. by Richard Rudinski. Addison, 1979.
Photographs and simple text combine to explain how Eric gets stitches.

Raskin, Ellen. *Spectacles*. Atheneum, 1968.
A young girl thinks she sees dragons and other unusual things until she discovers she needs glasses.

Rey, Margaret. *Curious George Goes to the Hosptial*. Houghton Mifflin, 1966.
Common hospital experiences are depicted, including descriptions of injections, nurses, x-rays, operating rooms, anesthesia procedures, and feelings of loneliness.

Robison, Deborah, and Carla Perez. *Your Turn Doctor*. Illus. by Deborah Robison. Dial, 1982.
This story may take some of the fear out of visiting a doctor. In its humorous reversal of roles, a little girl becomes a doctor, and the adult doctor, the patient.

Rockwell, Anne, and Harlow Rockwell. *The Emergency Room*. Macmillan, 1985.
Practices and procedures of a typical emergency room are described by a young boy who is there for a sprained ankle.

Sharmat, Marjorie W. *I Want Mama*. Walck, 1975.
When a mother goes to the hospital for surgery, her young daughter experiences anger, loneliness, and anxiety until she realizes her mother will be home soon.

Sobol, Harriet. *Jeff's Hospital Book*. Walck, 1975.
Young Jeff is having an operation to have his eyes straightened. Black-and-white photographs and careful text explain hospital procedures to relieve anxiety about a visit.

Waber, Bernard. *Lyle and the Birthday Party*. Houghton Mifflin, 1966.
When Lyle, a crocodile, starts acting and looking strange, his family calls in a doctor who sends him to a hospital. A humorous story, with some hospital procedures briefly described.

Wolde, Gunilla. *Betsy and the Chicken Pox*. Random, 1976.
For Betsy, being sick looks like fun especially when you get a lot of attention. She finds out differently when she comes down with chicken pox.

V. DIVORCE

Divorce is a stressful situation and is often found to be as traumatic as death. There are many books to help children understand their emotions about this new family situation.

Caines, Jeanette. *Daddy*. Illus. by Ronald Himler. Harper, 1977.
Windy and her father have a very special relationship although she only sees him on weekends.

Goff, Beth. *Where Is Daddy? The Story of Divorce*. Illus. by Susan Perl. Beacon, 1969.
Until her mother and father reassure her that they love her, Janey's anger and confusion over her parents' divorce are expressed in a variety of ways, including hitting her dog.

Hazen, Barbara. *Two Homes to Live In: A Child's Eye-View of Divorce*. Illus. by Peggy Luks. Human Sciences, 1978.
A child tells about the reasons for her parents' divorce and about her feelings, from guilt to fear, sadness, and anger.

Jukes, Mavis. *Like Jake and Me*. Random, 1984.
Humorous and touching story about a boy's growing relationship with his new stepfather.

Lexau, Joan. *Emily and the Klunky Baby and the Next-Door Dog*. Dial, 1972.
Since her parents' divorce, Emily feels that her mother is too busy and doesn't want her or her baby sister anymore.

Lindsay, Jeanne. *Do I Have a Daddy?* Illus. by DeeDee U. Warr. Morning Glory Press, 1982.
A story about a boy who wonders why he never sees his father. An appended section for single parents gives suggestions on how to talk to children about their "special father."

Perry, Patricia, and Marietta Lynch. *Mommy and Daddy Are Divorced*. Dial, 1978.
Large photos and first-person narrative convey Ned's anger and divided loyalties after his parents' divorce.

Rogers, Helen. *Morris and His Brave Lion*. McGraw, 1975.
A tender story of a boy's sadness over his parents' divorce. His father's gift of a toy lion helps the boy find his own courage.

Schuchman, Joan. *Two Places to Sleep*. Illus. by Jim LaMarche. Carolrhoda, 1985.

David describes living with his father and visiting his mother on weekends after his parents' divorce.

VI. SOME SPECIAL HANDICAPS

Recently, more books about handicaps have been published for younger children. Learning about these handicaps dispels fear and brings more understanding.

Brown, Tricia. *Someone Special Just like You*. Photos by Fran Ortiz. Holt, 1984.
    Black-and-white photographs and simple text show how children with handicaps are alike and also different from children without handicaps.
Fox, Mem. *Wilfrid Gordon McDonald Partridge*. Illus. by Julie Vivas. Miller, 1985.
    A young boy develops a special relationship with an old woman who has lost her memory.
Jensen, Virginia A. *Catching*. Philomel, 1983.
    In this simple, textured story, Little Rough and Little Shaggy are playing tag. For both blind and sighted children.
Kirk, Barbara. *Grandpa, Me and Our House in the Tree*. Macmillan, 1978.
    A boy and his grandfather have fun building a tree house together until grandfather has a stroke. They learn, however, that there are still many things that they can share together.
Lasker, Joe. *Nick Joins In*. Whitman, 1980.
    Going to a new "regular" school is frightening for Nick who is confined to a wheelchair. He and his new classmates soon find that they have much to learn from one another.
Peterson, Jeanne. *I Have a Sister, My Sister Is Deaf*. Illus. by Deborah Ray. Harper, 1977.
    This poetic story describes how a deaf sister relates differently to the world.
Prall, Jo. *My Sister's Special*. Photos by Linda Gray. Childrens Press, 1985.
    Although Angie cannot walk, talk, or use her hands because she is brain-damaged, she goes to school and enjoys life in a loving family.
Rosenberg, Maxine B. *My Friend Leslie: The Story of a Handicapped Child*. Photos by George Ancona. Lothrop, 1983.
    Leslie is a multi-handicapped kindergartener whose classmates learn to accept and appreciate her differences.
Wahl, Jan. *Jamie's Tiger*. Harcourt, 1978.
    German measles left Jamie with a hearing impairment, and he learns to finger-spell and wear a hearing aid.

Wolf, Bernard. *Anna's Silent World*. Harper, 1977.
Superb black-and-white photographs document the active life of Anna, who lives in New York City with her family.

VII. DEATH AND DYING

Most children experience the death of a pet and, sometimes, the death of a loved one. There are many books to help with the bereavement process.

Aliki. *Two of Them*. Greenwillow, 1979.
When Grandpa dies, the child sits in his orchard and thinks of the blossoms to come.

Bartoli, Jennifer. *Nonna*. Harvey House, 1975.
Two youngsters whose grandmother dies take an active part in the funeral and burial and are allowed to express their emotions.

Brown, Margaret Wise. *The Dead Bird*. Harper, 1958.
Some children find a dead bird and conduct a child-like funeral for it. They return to the burial site until they forget and go back to their regular activities.

Burningham, John. *Granpa*. Crown, 1985.
A little girl has a joyous relationship with her grandfather. Death is shown only by Granpa's empty chair at the book's end.

Carrick, Carol. *The Accident*. Illus. by Donald Carrick. Houghton Mifflin, 1976.
A truck accidentally kills Christopher's dog while he's taking him for a walk. He overcomes his anger and grief with his father's help.

Caseley, Judith. *When Grandpa Came to Stay*. Greenwillow, 1986.
When Grandma dies, Grandpa comes to live at Benny's house. Grandpa and Benny enjoy each other's company and both learn about grieving.

Cazet, Denys. *Christman Moon*. Bradbury, 1984.
Little Rabbit and his grandmother remember happy times when Grandpa was alive.

Clifton, Lucille. *Everett Anderson's Good-Bye*. Illus by Ann Grifalconi. Holt, 1983.
A young boy's reaction to his father's death is shown through poetry and pictures.

Coutant, Helen. *First Snow*. Illus. by Vo-Dinh. Knopf, 1974.
Young Lien sees dying as a natural process, a change like the beginning and end of a snowflake.

dePaola, Tomie. *Nana Upstairs and Nana Downstairs*. Putnam, 1973.
Tommy's great-grandmother dies, and he learns that he can bring her back in his memory merely by thinking of her.

Dobrin, Arnold. *Scat*. Four Winds, 1971.
Scat is able to express his feelings about his dead grandmother by playing his harmonica at her grave.

Fassler, Joan. *My Grandpa Died Today*. Illus. by Stewart Kranz. Human Sciences, 1971.
Because Grandpa has prepared him, David is able to cope with his grandfather's death, comforted that Grandpa would want him to be happy.

Miles, Miska. *Annie and the Old One*. Illus. by Peter Parnall. Little, 1971.
Annie's Navajo grandmother explains that she will return to earth when she finishes weaving a rug. Annie tries to unravel the rug to stop death, but Grandmother explains that death is natural.

Peavy, Linda. *Allison's Grandfather*. Scribner, 1981.
Erica learns about death when her friend's grandpa dies. It is comforting for Erica to think of him riding over the mountains rather than lying dead.

Stein, Sara B. *About Dying: An Open Family Book for Parents and Children Together*. Walker, 1984.
With separate texts for parents and children, this book suggests answers to anticipated questions.

Tobias, Tobi. *Petey*. Westminster, 1973.
Emily is saddened by the death of her pet gerbil Petey.

Varley, Susan. *Badger's Parting Gifts*. Lothrop, 1984.
Each of Badger's friends remembers a special skill that Badger taught them before he died.

Viorst, Judith. *The Tenth Good Thing about Barney*. Illus. by Eric Blegvad. Atheneum, 1971.
When Barney the cat dies, its owner searches for good things to say about it.

Zolotow, Charlotte. *My Grandson Lew*. Harper, 1974.
Mother and son share memories of Grandpa.

VIII. PROFESSIONAL RESOURCES

The following professional resources are subject guides to books on special needs.

Bernstein, Joanne E. *Books to Help Children Cope with Separation and Loss*. 2nd ed. Bowker, 1983.
————.————. v.3. Bowker, 1989.

Cuddigan, Maureen, and Mary Beth Hanson. *Growing Pains: Helping Children Deal with Everyday Problems through Reading*. American Library Association, 1988.

Dreyer, Sharon Spredemann. *Bookfinder: A Guide to Children's Literature about the Needs and Problems of Youth Aged 2–15*. American Guidance Service, 1977.

————.————. v.2. American Guidance Service, 1981.

————. *Bookfinder: When Kids Need Books*. v.3. American Guidance Service, 1985.

————. *Bookfinder*. v.4. American Guidance Service, 1989.

Hirsch, Elizabeth. *Problems of Early Childhood: An Annotated Bibliography*. Garland, 1983.

Lima, Carolyn W., and John A. Lima. *A to Zoo: Subject Access to Children's Picture Books*. 3rd ed. Bowker, 1989.

McGovern, Edyth M. *They're Never Too Young for Books*. Mar Vista, 1980.

Yonkers Public Library, Children's Services. *Guide to Subjects and Concepts in Picture Book Format*. Oceana, 1974.

Subject Index

compiled by
Carol Nielsen

ABC books, 59
Adoption: bibliography, 90
Adventure books, 41
Alliteration, 3
Alphabet books, 9–10, 59; illustrations, 10
Attention span, 38, 42
Authors and illustrators, 48

Babies: and book use, 2, 7–8, 35–36, 35–37, 49–51; first books, 72; handling books, 73
Babysitters, 80, 84
Bible stories and prayers, 75, 80–81
Bibliographies: adoption, 90; books for preschoolers, 55; books for toddlers, 54; books for young children, 53–55; books on special subjects, 55; death and dying, 94–95; divorce, 92–93; doctor visits, 90–92; fingerplays, 61; for circle time, 59–61; gift books, 73–74; handicaps, 93–94; hospital visits, 90–92; morality, 85–86; moving, 84; new babies, 88–90; nursery school, 79; parent resources, 44–46; poetry, 62–63; religion and morality, 81
Bibliographies as handouts, 31
Bibliotherapy, 87, 88
Board books, 8, 30, 36, 50–51, 54
Book display, 21–22, 29, 73, 75, 87
Book selection, 1; bibliographies to guide parents, 72; guidelines for gift books, 71–72; how to choose gift books, 70–73; picture books, 11–12; rhyme books, 5
Booklists: as handouts, 19, 31, 32
Books: as gifts, 3, 70–74; for older children, 61; handling, 73; longer plots, 60; role of parents, 29; use in circle time, 59–61; where to buy, 72
Bookstores, 30
Booktalks, 31, 50; booklist to use, 41–44; for daycare providers, 49–53; presentation style, 57; resources for adults, 44–46
Butler, Dorothy, 33, 48

Child development, 1–2, 35; and imagination, 39; developing senses, 36–38; developmental stages, 35; imagination, 39; importance of books, 1–2, 70–71; importance of reading, 49; intelligence, 48; relating a child's experience, 60. See also Emotional development
Childcare. See Daycare providers
Children and book use, 8–9
Children's Book Week, 70
Circle time, 56, 57–59; booktalk and resources, 57–69
Clip art, 19–20
Cloth books (soft), 30

Concept books, 9–10, 37, 39, 51, 54, 59
Copyright–free illustrations, 19–20
Counting books, 59
Counting rhymes, 4
Counting songs, 6
Creative dramatics, 58–59; bibliography, 62–69
Cultural differences, 78, 83
Cumulative plots, 11–12, 60

Daycare, 79, 83
Daycare providers, 14, 33, 47, 56; booktalks, 47–53; using songs, 6
Death and dying: bibliography, 94–95
Death of a pet: bibliography, 79–80, 84; books about, 79–80
Designing handouts, 19–21
Developing senses, 36
Development. *See* Child development
Displaying books, 21–22
Divorce: bibliography, 92–93
Doctor visits: bibliography, 90–92
Drama: use with preschoolers, 58–59

Emotional development: books, 82–84; books on special problems, 55; comfort with familiar things, 39; curiousity, 40; expressing feelings, 77; fairness, 40; fostered by reading, 76–78; security and reading, 39–40; sense of accomplishment, 38–39, 40; special subjects picture books, 52
Ethical education of children: adult resources, 85–86; and book use, 75–86
Evaluation: forms, 24–27; promotional program, 24–25
Expectant parents, 29
Expressing feelings, 77, 82

Fairy tales, 40
Family Caregiver Association, 47
Family caregivers. *See* Daycare providers
Family relationships, 77–78, 82–83

Fear in young children, 77, 79
Films: to supplement booktalks, 56, 57; use in circle time, 56, 57
Fingerplays, 4, 6, 49–50; bibliography, 61–63; in circle time, 57–58
Flannel board storytelling, 56
Flannel boards: resources, 66–69
Folk tales, 60
Friendship, 83; in picture books, 78

Games, 9, 31; resources, 62–69
Gift books: bibliography, 73–74
Gift–giving and books, 3
Goals and objectives for programs, 14
Grants to buy extra materials, 19
Graphic design of handouts, 19–21

Handicaps: bibliography, 93–94
Handouts, 19–21
Hearing: reading aloud, 36
History books, 40
Home libraries, 35, 70–71, 72–73
Hospital visits: bibliography, 90–92
Humor in books, 41, 60

I Spy books, 8–9, 51, 54
Illustrations, 12, 51, 71; as art, 71; books for babies, 7; concept books, 9; importance in picture books, 71; Mother Goose, 3; short books, 10
Imagination, 39
Infants. *See* Babies
Information books, 11, 52, 55
Intelligence and reading, 48

Kidstamps Company of Ohio, 20

Language development, 35–36, 37, 38, 40–41; reading aloud, 37; in three-year-olds, 38–39
Larrick, Nancy, 33, 48
Libraries at home, 72
Lift–the–flap books, 10–11
Lullabies, 2, 6

Magazines, 31
Manual dexterity: handling books, 37

Morality: resource list, 85–86

Mother Goose, 2–5, 6, 36, 37, 49–50, 53, 59

Mother Goose books, 53

Moving, 79, 84

Name tags, 20

Naming books, 8–9

Naming objects, 36–37

National Council of Teachers of English, 33

Needs assessment, 13–14

Negativism, 37

New babies, 84; booklist, 88–90

New baby in the family, 79

Newspaper and newsletters as promotion tools, 22–23

Nonsense books, 38

Numbers. *See* Counting

Nursery rhymes, 2–5, 49–50, 53, 59

Nursery schools, 14; books about, 79

Object identification books, 30, 36

Onomatopoeia, 3

Opposites books, 9

Panorama books, 40–41

Parent resources, 44–48

Parents: and books, 29; guidelines for choosing books, 71–72

Participation books, 11, 51, 54

Photographs for promotions, 23

Picture books, 7, 10–11, 38, 40–41, 50–51, 54, 55; circle time, 57; for special needs, 87; for use with preschoolers, 52–53; for use with toddlers, 51; longer length, 11–12, 55; on special subjects, 52–53; use with preschoolers, 57; wordless, 55

Picture song books, 10, 11, 60

Pictures not in books, 31

Play rhymes, 4–5

Poetry, 38; and songs, 6; bibliography, 62–63

Prayer books, 84–85

Prayers, 80–81

Preparation for presentations, 15

Preschoolers: and books, 38–41; reading readiness, 33

Problem-solving books, 55, 78–80

Programs: audience, 13, 14, 23; babies and toddlers, 1–2; evaluation, 24–27; follow–up details, 27–28; goals and objectives, 14; ideas, 13–14; identifying target audience, 14; locations, 16; materials, 19; Mother Goose, 3–4; organization, 13; planning checklist, 16, 17–18; presentation style, 15, 21; rhyme books, 4–5, 5; scheduling, 16; song books, 6–7; supplementary materials, 21–22; surveying participants, 13–14; titles, 14–15; topics, 13–14

Promotion, 14–15, 22–27, 47–48

Public library: as provider of children's books, 30, 35, 47

Public relations, 22–27; evaluation, 24–25

Puppets: bibliography, 62–69; in circle time, 62–63

Questions by program audience, 22

Radio publicity, 23

Reading: aloud, 12, 31, 32, 33–35, 36, 56, 76; importance for development, 35–41; readiness, 9, 12, 33–35, 34–35, 76; with the look say method, 30

Reference tools, 5

Refreshments, 20–21

Religious education: adult books, 85–86; and book use, 75–86; introducing the Bible and prayers, 80–81

Rhyme books, 53

Rhymes, 2–5; and action play, 4–5; books, 50; *See also* Nursery rhymes; Play rhymes

Rogers, Fred, 79

Rubber stamps, 20

Scheduling programs, 16, 48

School, 79, 83

Science books, 40

Security objects: books about, 80

Self–concept: explored in reading, 76–77

Self–concept books, 82

Self–esteem: developed with book use, 39

Senses: development with reading, 36–41

Separation anxiety, 80, 84

Shape books, 9

Sibling rivalry, 79, 84; bibliography, 88–90

Song books, 5–7, 36, 39, 53, 60; bibliography, 63–69

Songs, 2, 5–7, 49–50

Special needs: how books help, 87, 88; picture books, 52–53, 55; 12; professional resources, 95–96

Storytelling: bibliography, 66–69; puppets and circle time, 58

Sunday school class, 81

Suspense books, 41

Teaching reading, 34

Television publicity, 23

Thank–you notes, 28

Thumbsucking, 84; books about, 80

Toddlers: and books, 1, 37–38; attention span, 38

Toilet training, 78, 83

Values education, 82, 87; role of books and reading, 76–78

Verbal development, 40–41

Vision: development with book use, 36

Vocabulary building, 3, 12

Wordless books, 40, 52, 55

Young children. *See* Preschoolers; Toddlers

Title Index

compiled by
Carol Nielsen

A-B-Cing: An Action Alphabet, 37, 41

A to Z Picture Book, 9, 51, 54

A to Zoo: Subject Access to Children's Picture Books, 75, 81, 96

Abby, 90

ABC, 59

ABC: An Alphabet Book, 73

About Dying: An Open Family Book for Parents and Children Together, 95

Accident, 79, 84

The Accident, 94

Across the Stream, 7, 50

The Adventures of Paddy Pork, 12, 52, 55

Airport, 11, 52, 55

Albert's Toothache, 82

Alfie Gets In First, 60, 76, 82

Alfie Gives a Hand, 52, 55, 84

Alfie's Feet, 39, 42

All Asleep, 72, 73

All Fall Down, 36, 43

All Kinds of Families, 77, 83

Allison's Grandfather, 95

Animal ABC, 36, 44

Animal Noises, 36, 43

Animals Should Definately Not Wear Clothes, 60

Anna's Silent World, 94

Annie and the Old One, 95

Anno's Counting Book, 59

Apples, 40, 42

Are There Hippos on the Farm?, 36, 43

Ask Mr. Bear, 12, 67, 73

Babar's Anniversary Album, 73

Babies Need Books, 32, 33, 44, 48

A Baby Sister for Frances, 89

Baby's Catalogue, 36, 41

The Baby's Lap Book, 72, 73

The Baby's Storybook, 72, 73

Badger's Parting Gifts, 95

Bags Are Big: A Paper Bag Craft Book, 65

Bear and Mrs. Duck, 80, 84

Bear Party, 83

Bear's Moving Day, 79

Bedtime for Frances, 52, 55

Being Adopted, 90

Benny Bakes a Cake, 10, 38, 45, 51, 54

The Berenstain Bears and the Sitter, 80, 84

The Berenstain Bears and the Truth, 82

Betsy and the Chicken Pox, 92

Bible Stories for Children, 80, 84

A Big Fat Enormous Lie, 82

Big Learning for Little Learners: Easy Guide for Teaching Early Childhood Activities, 66

The Blanket That Had to Go, 80, 84

Blue Sea, 39, 43

Blueberries for Sal, 60

Boat Book, 40, 42

Bookfinder, 96

Bookfinder: A Guide to Children's Literature about the Needs and Problems of Youth Aged 2-15, 75, 81, 96

Bookfinder: When Kids Need Books, 96

Booksharing: 101 Programs to Use with Preschoolers, 67

A Boy, a Dog and a Frog, 52, 55

Brian Wildsmith's ABC, 36, 44

Brian Wildsmith's Illustrated Bible Stories, 80, 85

Brian Wildsmith's Mother Goose, 53

Brothers Are All the Same, 90

Brown Bear, Brown Bear, What Do You See?, 7, 38, 45, 50, 54, 73

Building a House, 11, 52, 55

Bye Bye, Old Buddy, 80, 84

The Cake That Mack Ate, 38, 44

Caps for Sale, 60

The Cat Goes Fiddle-i-Fee, 39, 42

Catch Me and Kiss Me and Say It Again, 5

Catching, 93

Catherine Marshall's Story Bible, 84

Celebrate! Holidays, Puppets and Creative Drama, 64

A Chair for My Mother, 61

The Chick and the Duckling, 82

A Child Is Born: The Christmas Story, 81, 85

Children's Faces Looking Up: Program Building for the Storyteller, 67

A Children's Zoo, 52, 55

A Child's Book of Prayers, 81, 85

Choosing Books for Children: A Commonsense Guide, 45, 72

Choosing Books for Kids: Choosing the Right Book for the Right Child at the Right Time, 46

Chosen Baby, 90

Christman Moon, 94

Circus Baby, 76, 82

Claude and Pepper, 40, 42, 77, 82

Clip-Art Book of Cartoon Style Illustrators, 20

Clip Book Number 10: Shapes, Frames and Borders, 20

Clipper Creative Art Service, 20

Clyde Monster, 77, 83

Colors, 36, 43

The Complete Book of Baby and Child Care for Christian Parents, 81, 85

Corduroy, 39, 42, 60, 67, 73

Crash! Bang! Boom!, 36, 44

Creepy Castle, 40, 42

Crictor, 41, 44

Curious George, 74

Curious George Goes to the Hospital, 91

Cut and Tell Scissor Stories for Fall, 69

Cut and Tell Scissor Stories for Spring, 69

Cut and Tell Scissor Stories for Winter, 69

Daddy, 92

Dandelion, 39, 42, 76, 82

David Decides about Thumbsucking: A Motivating Story for Children: An Informative Guide for Parents, 80, 84

The Dead Bird, 94

Dear Zoo, 37, 38, 42

Dinosaurs Divorce: A Guide for Changing Families, 53, 55

Do I Have a Daddy?, 92

Do Your Ears Hang Low?, 63

Doctor DeSoto, 61, 74

Doctors' Tools, 91

Each Peach Pear Plum, 38, 41

Early Childhood Literature Sharing Programs in Libraries, 45

Early Words, 37, 44

The Emergency Room, 91

Emily and the Klunky Baby and the Next-Door Dog, 92

Eric Need Stitches, 91

Everett Anderson's Good-Bye, 94

Everett Anderson's Nine Months Long, 53, 55

Every Time I Climb a Tree, 38, 43

The Everything Book: For Teachers of Young Children, 64, 66

Eye Winker, Tom Tinker, Chin Chopper: Fifty Musical Fingerplays, 6, 49, 53, 61, 63, 72, 73

Father Fox's Pennyrhymes, 5

Feelings, 77, 82

Felt Board Fun, 66

Finger Rhymes, 61, 63

Fire Engines, 11, 52, 55

The Fireside Book of Children's Songs, 6, 49, 53

A First Bible, 80, 84

First Prayers, 81, 85

First Snow, 94

The Flannel Board Storybook, 68

The Flannel Board Storytelling Book, 68

A Folk Lullaby, 60

For Reading Out Loud! A Guide to Sharing Books with Children, 67

Frederick, 82

Freight Train, 10, 38, 42, 51, 54, 59, 71, 73

Friends, 51, 54

From Hand to Head, 65

Games and How to Play Them, 65

Games for Reading: Playful Ways to Help Your Child Read, 45

Games for the Very Young: Finger Plays and Nursery Games, 64

Georgia Music, 78, 83

Getting Ready to Read, 44

The Gingerbread Boy, 12

Glad Rags: Stories and Activities Featuring Clothes for Preschool Children, 67

Glove, Mitten and Sock Puppets, 62

Gobble Growl Grunt, 9, 51, 54

Going to Day Care, 53, 55, 79, 83

Going to the Potty, 53, 55, 78, 83

Goldilocks and the Three Bears, 73

Good Books to Grow On: A Guide to

Building Your Child's Library from Birth to Age Five, 45, 72

Goodnight, Moon, 7, 40, 42, 50, 73

Goodnight Owl, 12

The Gorilla Did It, 82

Grandpa, Me and Our House in the Tree, 93

Granpa, 94

Great Big Animal Book, 44

The Great Big Animal Book, 37

A Great Big Enormous Lie, 77

The Greedy Shopkeeper, 77, 82

Gregory Griggs and Other Nursery Rhyme People, 59

Growing Pains: Helping Children Deal with Everyday Problems through Reading, 75, 81, 95

Guide to Subjects and Concepts in Picture Book Format, 96

Gunniwolf, 40, 42, 58, 60

Hand Rhymes, 61

Handbook for Storytellers, 67

Happy Birthday, Sam, 60

Harriet's Recital, 82

Harry the Dirty Dog, 11, 39, 44, 74

The Hating Book, 77, 82

The Helen Oxenbury Nursery Story Book, 72, 73

Helping Your Child Learn Right from Wrong: A Guide to Values Clarification, 81, 86

Holes and Peeks, 77, 82

How Do I Put It On?, 37, 44, 51, 54

How My Parents Learned to Eat, 78, 83

How to Choose Books for Kids, 46

Hush Little Baby: A Folk Lullaby, 10, 36, 41, 50, 54

I Don't Want to Go to School, 79, 83

I Have a Sister, My Sister Is Deaf, 93

I Love My Baby Sister (Most of the Time), 88

I Read Signs, 59

I Saw a Purple Cow, 63

I Spy: A Picture Book of Objects in a

Child's Home Environment, 8, 36, 43, 51, 54
I Want a Brother or Sister, 89
I Want Mama, 91
I Wish I Was Sick Too!, 77, 82
In My Garden, 40, 43
Ira Sleeps Over, 80, 84
Is That Your Sister? A True Story of Adoption, 90
It Looked like Spilt Milk, 11, 38, 44, 59
It's a Baby!, 79, 84, 88
It's Not Fair, 77

Jafta's Mother, 78, 83
Jamberry, 12, 38, 42
Jamie's Tiger, 93
Jeff's Hospital Book, 91
Jim and the Beanstalk, 41, 42
Jim's Dog Muffins, 79, 84
Jonah and the Great Fish, 81, 85
Joseph and His Brothers, 81, 85
Juba This and Juba That: Story Hour Stretches for Large and Small Groups, 61, 68
Jumanji, 12, 41, 44, 61
Just Me and My Dad, 77, 83

Katharine's Doll, 78, 83
Kids' Stuff Book of Patterns, Projects and Plans to Perk Up Early Learning, 63
Kidstamps Catalog, 20
King Bidgood's in the Bathtub, 60
Kitten Up a Tree, 39, 43
Knee Baby, 89

The Lady with the Alligator Purse, 39, 44, 60
The Laughing Baby: Remembering Nursery Rhymes and Reasons, 5
The Learning Child, 45
Learning through Play, 64
Leo the Late Bloomer, 82
Let Loose on Mother Goose, 64
Let's Do Fingerplays, 61
Like Jake and Me, 92

Lisa Cannot Sleep, 38, 41
Listen and Help Tell the Story, 67
Little Blue and Little Yellow, 9
The Little Girl and the Big Bear, 40, 42
Look Around! A Book about Shapes, 39, 42
Look What I Can Do, 82
Lots More Tell and Draw Stories, 68
Lyle and the Birthday Party, 91

Madeline, 90
Make Way for Ducklings, 52, 55
Making Easy Puppets, 62
Making Glove Puppets, 62
Making Puppets Come Alive: A Method of Learning and Teaching Hand Puppetry, 62
Marguerite De Angeli's Book of Nursery and Mother Goose Rhymes, 53
Mary Had a Little Lamb, 42
Mary Wore Her Red Dress, 39, 43
Max's New Suit, 37, 44
May We Sleep Here Tonight?, 41, 43
Miffy in the Hospital, 91
Mike Mulligan and His Steam Shovel, 39, 42
Millions of Cats, 60, 73
Mine's the Best, 78, 83
Miss Nelson Is Missing, 61
Mitchell Is Moving, 79, 84
Mitt Magic: Fingerplays for Finger Puppets, 65
Molly's Lie, 77, 82
Mommy and Daddy Are Divorced, 92
Moon Came Too, 40
The Moon Came Too, 42
Moonlight, 55
Moral Development: A Guide to Piaget and Kohlberg, 81, 85
Moral Life of Children, 81, 85
More Tell and Draw Stories, 68
Morning, Rabbit, Morning, 7
Morris and His Brave Lion, 92
The Most Amazing Hide-and-Seek Alphabet Book, 38, 42
The Mother Goose Treasury, 53

Mother Goose: A Collection of Classic Nursery Rhymes, 53
The Mother Goose Book, 53
Mother Goose Treasurey, 36, 42
Move Over, Mother Goose: Finger Plays, Action Verses and Funny Rhymes, 63
Moving, 79, 84
Mr. Gumpy's Outing, 10, 37, 42, 51, 54
Mudluscious: Stories and Activities Featuring Food for Preschool Children, 67
Muppets in My Neighborhood, 37, 44
Music for Ones and Twos: Songs and Games for the Very Young, 64
My Barber, 39, 44
My Day on the Farm, 37, 43
My Dentist, 53, 55
My Doctor, 53, 55
My Friend Leslie: The Story of a Handicapped Child, 93
My Grandpa Died Today, 95
My Grandson Lew, 95
My Mamma Needs Me, 90
My Name Is Emily, 89
My Nursery School, 79, 83
My Sister's Special, 93

Nana Upstairs and Nana Downstairs, 94
Napping House, 38, 44
New Baby, 89
A New Baby, 88
The New Baby at Your House, 53, 55
The New Read-Aloud Handbook, 46
The New York Times Parent's Guide to the Best Books for Children, 46
Nick Joins In, 93
No More Diapers, 78, 83
Noah and the Ark, 81, 85
Nobody Asked Me If I Wanted a Baby Sister, 79, 84, 88
Noisy Nora, 39, 44, 90
Nonna, 94
Not So Fast, Songololo, 78, 83

Numbers of Things, 36, 43
Nutshell Library, 72, 74

Of Colors and Things, 51, 54
Oh, A-Hunting We Will Go, 11, 60
On Market Street, 59, 73
On Mother's Lap, 40, 44, 89
The Once-upon-a-Time Dragon, 41, 43
One, Two, Three, 72, 73
101 Things to Do with a Baby, 78, 83, 89
One Hunter, 38, 42, 71, 73
Our Cat Flossie, 37, 42
The Oxford Nursery Rhymes Book, 5

The Pain and the Great One, 77, 82
Paper Stories, 66
Parenting for Peace and Justice, 81, 86
A Parent's Guide to Children's Reading, 45, 48
Pat the Bunny, 31, 43, 72, 73
Peace at Last, 59, 60
Peace in the Family, 81, 86
Pecos Bill, 12
Peek-a-Boo!, 9, 51, 54
People, 78, 83
Peter's Chair, 60, 79, 83, 89
Petey, 95
Pickle Things, 41, 42
Picture Book Story Hours: From Birthdays to Bears, 68
Picture Books for Children, 45
Pig Pig Grows Up, 41, 43
The Playgroup Handbook, 63
Playing, 51, 54
Playing with Puppets, 62
Poems to Read to the Very Young, 38, 43
Pooh's Bedtime Book, 73
The Potpourri: Clip Book of Line Artwork, 20
Prayer for a Child, 81, 85
Problems of Early Childhood: An Annotated Guide, 87, 96
Puppet Fun, 62
Puppet Party, 62

Puppetry and Creative Dramatics in Storytelling, 62, 67

Puppetry in Early Childhood Education, 62, 64

Puppets for Beginners, 62

Puppets with Pizazz: 52 Finger and Hand Puppets Children Can Make and Use, 63

Purple Cow to the Rescue, 63

Quick Clips: ALA Clip Art III, 20

The Rabbit, 37, 42

Rabbit's Morning, 50, 54

Raffi Singable Songbook, 65

Rain, 43, 59

Rain Makes Applesauce, 60

Raising Good Children: From Birth through the Teenage Years, 81, 86

Raising Readers: A Guide to Sharing Literature with Young Children, 33, 46

The Random House Book of Mother Goose: A Treasury of 306 Timeless Nursery Rhymes, 53

Read-Aloud Rhymes for the Very Young, 11, 38, 43, 74

Reading Begins at Home: Preparing Children for Reading before They Go to School, 45

The Real Mother Goose, 53, 59, 72, 74

Recipes for Art and Craft Materials, 66

Recipes for Creeping Crystals, Invisible Ink, Self-Stick Plastic, Grease Paint, Playdough and Other Inedibles, 65

Recipes for Fun and Learning: Creative Learning Activities for Young Children, 64

Red Riding Hood, 40, 43, 60

The Relatives Came, 60

Rhymes for Fingers and Flannelboards, 61, 66

Rhymes for Learning Times, 66

Richard Scarry's Best Word Book Ever, 41, 44

Ring a Ring o'Roses: Finger Plays for Preschool Children, 61, 65

Rosie's Walk, 59

Round Robin, 41, 43

The Runaway Bunny, 51, 54

Scat, 95

Scribble Cookies and Other Independent Creative Art Experiences for Children, 64

Sharon, Lois and Bram's Mother Goose, 36, 44

Shawn Goes to School, 60, 79, 83

She Come Bringing Me That Little Baby Girl, 88

Singing Bee! A Collection of Favorite Children's Songs, 6, 49, 53, 64

The Sky Is Full of Stars, 40, 41

Smart Times: A Parent's Guide to Quality Time with Preschoolers, 81, 85

Snakes, 40, 43

Snow White and the Seven Dwarfs, 41, 42

The Snowy Day, 52, 55

Someone Special Just like You, 93

Spectacles, 91

Starting School, 79, 83

The Story of the Statue of Liberty, 40, 43

Story Programs: A Source Book of Materials, 68

Storytelling Activities, 67

Storytelling: Art and Technique, 66

Storytelling with Puppets, 62, 67

Storytelling with the Flannel Board, 66, 69

Storytimes for Two-Year-Olds, 56, 68

The Straw Maid, 40, 43

Sunshine, 12, 55

The Supermarket, 39, 44

Swimmy, 40, 43

Taking Books to Heart: How to Develop a Love of Reading in Your Child, 45

The Tale of Beatrix Potter, 43

The Tale of Peter Rabbit, 40, 74

The Tall Book of Mother Goose, 53

Taryn Goes to the Dentist, 91

Teaching Your Child to Make Decisions: How to Raise a Responsible Child, 81, 86

Teddy Bears' Moving Day, 84

The Teddy Bears' Picnic, 73

Tell and Draw Stories, 68

Tell Me Grandma, Tell Me Grandpa, 77, 83

Ten, Nine, Eight, 39, 41, 51, 54, 59

The Tenth Good Thing about Barney, 53, 55, 80, 84, 95

That New Baby: An Open Family Book for Parents and Children Together, 89

There Was an Old Lady Who Swallowed a Fly, 60

They're Never Too Young for Books, 96

Things I Like to Wear, 51, 54

This Little Pig Went to Market: Play Rhymes for Infants and Young Children, 4, 50, 53, 61

The Three Bears, 40, 42, 52, 55

Three Bears and Fifteen Other Stories, 41, 44

The Three Bears and Fifteen Other Stories, 74

The Three Billy Goats Gruff, 60, 73

Three Little Kittens, 42

Tikki Tikki Tembo, 41, 43

Timothy Goes to School, 78, 83

Titch, 38, 42, 51, 54

Tomie dePaola's Favorite Nursery Tales, 41, 42

Tomie dePaola's Mother Goose, 37, 42, 53, 59, 73

Ton and Pon: Big and Little, 76, 82

Trucks, 11, 52, 55

Twenty Tellable Tales: Audience Participation for the Beginning Storyteller, 68

Two Bear Cubs, 38, 43

Two Homes to Live In: A Child's Eye-View of Divorce, 92

Two of Them, 94

Two Places to Sleep, 92

Umbrella, 60

The Very Busy Spider, 71-72, 73

The Very Hungry Caterpillar, 9-10, 38, 42, 51, 54, 59, 72

The Very Worst Monster, 79, 83

The Village of the Round and Square Houses, 78, 83

Waiting for Jennifer, 79, 84

Watch the Stars Come Out, 40, 43

We Are Best Friends, 79, 84

Wee Sing: Children's Songs and Fingerplays, 58, 61, 63

We're Very Good Friends, My Brother and I, 78, 83

What Is It?, 73

What Sadie Sang, 60

What Shall We Do and Allee Galloo! Play Songs and Singing Games for Young Children, 66

What's So Great about Books, 57

Wheels on the Bus, 39, 43

When Grandpa Came to Stay, 94

When You Go to Kindergarten, 79, 83

Where Is Daddy? The Story of Divorce, 92

Where Is My Friend?, 39, 43

Where the Wild Things Are, 52, 55, 60, 71, 74

Where's Spot?, 10, 37, 42, 51, 54, 56, 60, 72

Whistle for Willie, 11, 39, 43, 52, 55

Who's Counting, 38, 44

Whose Mouse Are You?, 39-40, 43

Wide-Awake Timothy, 38, 44

Wild Animals, 37, 44

Wiley and the Hairy Man, 60

Wilfrid Gordon McDonald Partridge, 93

Will I Have a Friend?, 78, 83

A Winter Day, 37, 42
With a Deep Sea Smile: Story Hour
    Stretches for Large and Small
    Groups, 68
The Wizard, the Fairy and the Magic
    Chicken, 78, 83
Wizard of Wallaby Wallow, 77, 82
Won't Somebody Play with Me?, 83

Would You Rather?, 56, 60

You Do It Too, 37
You Go Away, 80, 84
Young Joe, 37, 43
Your Child at Play: One to Two
    Years, 46
Your Turn Doctor, 91